Trauma
and the Twelve Steps

Steps

A COMPLETE
GUIDE TO
ENHANCING
RECOVERY

Jamie Marich Ph.D.

 Cornersburg Media

Disclaimer :

This book does not intend to be diagnostic in any way and is not a substitute for a thorough clinical assessment. If you are reading this book and feel that any of the problems herein apply to you personally, you are encouraged to seek out an assessment from a qualified professional as soon as possible. If you are at medical risk of withdrawal or in a serious psychiatric emergency (e.g., suicidal or homicidal ideations), you are encouraged to present for medical attention immediately.

Trauma and the Twelve Steps:
A Complete Guide to Enhancing Recovery

© Cornersburg Media Warren OH, USA, 2012

ISBN # 978-0615603056

All author photography by Ellen DeCarlo

www.jamiemarich.com
www.drjamiemarich.com
www.TraumaTwelve.com

Book summary: Criticism of 12-step recovery is nothing new; however, 12-step programs are increasingly getting a bad rap for being too "one size fits all," or not applicable to individuals struggling with issues beyond the scope of simple alcoholism or addiction, especially issues surrounding traumatic stress. Trauma and the Twelve Steps: A Complete Guide to Enhancing Recovery takes the posture that there is nothing wrong with using 12-step recovery principles in treatment or in continuing care with individuals who are affected by trauma-related issues. However, this book also explains how rigid application of 12-step principles can do more harm than good for a traumatized person, and that learning some simple accommodations based on the latest knowledge of traumatic stress can enhance the 12-step recovery experiences for trauma survivors. Written for professionals, sponsors, and those in a position to reach out and help recovering addicts, the user-friendly language in this book will teach you how to unify the traditional knowledge of 12-step recovery with the latest findings on healing trauma. In doing so, you will be able to help others, and maybe even yourself, "work a recovery" program like never before!

ISBN: 061560305X
ISBN 13: 9780615603056

Library of Congress Control Number: 2012933824
CreateSpace, North Charleston, SC

For Janet L.

Because you worked your eleventh and twelfth steps, I have the life I have today.
I am eternally grateful. . .

Table Of Contents

Acknowledgments

Getting this book to press has been a bit of an uphill battle. In preparing this manuscript for publication, I ran into the same struggles that I encounter working as a clinician in the helping professions. Mental health publishers felt that this book was "too addiction." Addiction publishers felt it was "too mental health." Academic publishers called it too "colloquial," and self-help publishers too "academic." See why I call my company Cornersburg Media? I truly live on the juncture of so many different worlds! Because I am not labeling this as a traditional *co-occurring* disorders book, but rather, one that promotes a true bridging of the gap between the addiction recovery and mental health treatment approaches, others have deemed this book a *hard sell*. This book is not like others on trauma and addiction, because I'm not proposing a new model for care; we don't need any more models, we need true integration of our thinking. If you have picked up this book and are reading it now, I thank you for at least considering that this revolutionary view of recovery is what we must embrace in order to save lives.

I send my deepest and sincerest thanks to the people in my inner circle of support who have never ceased to believe in what I have to say: Allison Bugzavich, Rev. Betsy Schenk, Janet L., Denise Sudano, Amber Stiles-Bodnar, Linda Curran, Ellen DeCarlo, Brandy Bates, Jeff Sanders, Kathy Barecca, Todd Maki, Maureen Lauer-Gatta, Dr. Erica Matthews, Leisa M., Kara Mazey, Eric DiBell, Clayton Manning, Mary Riley, Claire Taylor, Dr. Earl Grey, William Tipton, David Reiter, Paul Marich. Collectively, your encouragement gave me the push I needed to bring this book, in its current form, into existence.

Professionally, I am indebted to my entire family at PsyCare, Inc., especially Dr. Douglas Darnall, Kathy Dix, Mary Wargo, and Mary Beth Hayer—words cannot express how grateful I am for your support and your faith in me as a clinician, trainer, and writer. Thank you for your flexibility and willingness to work with my crazy schedule.

I also owe a great debt of professional gratitude to my family at CMI Education/Premiere Education and Media for having the faith to send me out on the road and support my trainings nationally; it was on the road that I conceived of the idea for this book in the first place. A special, heartfelt acknowledgement goes out to Linda Jackson, whose steadfast support of my addiction training topics has continued to fuel me. I also send thanks out to my various teachers and trainers over the years, especially those within the EMDR community who have supported my outspoken nature. As a great friend in this community once made me realize, we can't change the world by living in the status quo.

Thank you to Dr. Lisa Najavits for her invaluable feedback as I prepared the final manuscript.

Most importantly, my thanks go out to my clients and my friends in recovery that I have had the privilege of working with and knowing over the years. The experience of having you in my life, sharing the gifts of recovery with you, and having gifts shared with me in return comes through in all of my training and writing. With a grateful heart, I thank each of you!

CHAPTER **I**

The Problem with the "They're Just Addicts" Mentality (an Introduction)

It takes a special person to work with alcoholics and addicts, whether you serve in some professional capacity at a treatment center, or whether you do it as a member of a twelve-step or other fellowship program. Before you read another word of this book, allow me to thank you for your service if you are one of these people. Many of us would agree that working with those who suffer from the disease of addiction is more than just a job; it's a vocation. The reason I say *it takes a special person* is that the joy of helping someone recover often comes with frustration. There are those who outright don't want recovery and make your job seem like a living hell. Perhaps the most heartbreak can come when you work with someone who seems to want recovery, and may even be giving it her all, but then inevitably relapses. Relapse is a mystifying phenomenon to understand, yet I would like to share a story with you that opened my eyes to what we may be missing.

I entered the field of addiction treatment treatment as a novice counselor, eager and excited to bring the gift of recovery to others. One of my first jobs was in a reputable treatment facility near my hometown. The high rate of relapse that I observed quickly disillusioned me. The amount of readmissions troubled me, and when clients complained that the treatment they received was "one size fits all," a large part of me found myself agreeing with them. When I talked to my senior colleagues about these phenomena, they placated me with responses like, "They're just addicts. Until they come to terms with their addiction and realize that they really want to treat their disease, they'll always be coming back." The one-size fits all complaint was addressed with, "Come on, Jamie, you know it's just their terminal uniqueness talking."

One day, I found occasion to consult with my clinical director about the high level of trauma-related problems I saw our clients struggling to address: sexual abuse, combat memories, horrific accidents, scars from growing up with alcoholic parents, and assaults. My clinical director warned me that I was getting offtrack from the real problem (i.e., the addiction) by paying so much attention to these issues. "They're here because they're addicts," he insisted. Ever the devil's advocate, I asked if he believed that the trauma had anything to do with it, and he immediately cut me off for complicating matters too much. Something inside of me signaled danger. Not only did I not agree with what he was telling me, I felt it was detrimental to our mission of helping others recover. I got personal in trying to state my case to this clinical director.

"Do you mean to tell me," I said, "that I picked up opiates at the age of twelve because things were good in my life?"

"You picked up opiates at the age of twelve because you are an addict," he quipped back. I was very saddened to hear his position, especially since, in my own early recovery, I was blessed with a series of trauma-sensitive treatment counselors. My counselor honored my history and my struggles with trauma, yet knew the competent balance of not letting me turn them into an excuse to prolong my addiction progression. She once told me, "Jamie, after everything you've been through, no wonder you turned out to be an addict. The question is, now, what are you going to do about it?" I found her philosophy incredibly balanced and life changing. I expand upon that balanced philosophy in this book as the ultimate avenue to being trauma-sensitive and trauma-informed in our execution of traditional twelve-step recovery principles.

Needless to say, I did not last very long working at this treatment center. I saw so many patients (who had initially taken to recovery like ducks to water) relapse, leave, and return when the really hard issues surfaced in their recovery. From my perspective, so much of it was about trauma. Not only major events like war and rape that we associate with post-traumatic stress disorder (PTSD), but also the life-changing events that never quite get resolved. Essentially, the things that keep us stuck in our shame. In the emphasis on "Don't drink and go to meetings" and "Challenge your faulty thinking" that dominated this treatment center's culture, they seemed to ignore many of the issues that blocked the attainment of recovery.

I don't mean my story to sound bitter about my first place of employment, or even about traditional twelve-step recovery. On the contrary, I am full of gratitude to this treatment center for opening my eyes to the issues that now define my clinical practice. The problems I encountered there exist in many treatment centers throughout North America. Rigid acceptance of the disease model of addiction and near-fundamentalist adherence to twelve-step philosophies can hurt more clients than they can help. Interestingly, I am not opposed to the disease model of addiction, and I am actually an adamant believer in the benefits of twelve-step programming for most people. This is not one of those books that seeks to challenge the relevance of twelve-step programs, or other approaches to recovery, in the modern era. Let me say it right here: I believe that any healthy approach to recovery that promotes genuine lifestyle change can work. The harm comes when we apply these philosophies at the exclusion of everything else that the fields of psychology, counseling, social work, and medicine have enlightened for us in the past several decades about the reality of trauma and its effects on human beings.

The purpose of this book is to show professionals, sponsors, and recovering individuals how to continue using traditional twelve-step recovery philosophies in a manner that honors what the psychotherapeutic professions have learned about traumatic stress. Criticism of twelve-step recovery is nothing new; however, twelve-step programs are increasingly getting a bad rap for being too "one size fits all" or not being applicable to individuals struggling with issues beyond the scope of simple alcoholism or addiction. This book takes the posture that there is nothing wrong with using twelve-step recovery principles in treatment or in continuing care with individuals affected by trauma-related issues. However, this book also explains how rigid application of twelve-step principles can do more harm than good for a traumatized person and how learning some simple accommodations based on the latest knowledge of traumatic stress can enhance the twelve-step recovery experience for trauma survivors.

As many of you who have picked up this book are aware, not all twelve-step fellowship meetings and twelve-step-oriented treatment programs are created equal. First of all, even though the twelve steps were published as a suggested plan of action by *Alcoholics Anonymous* (AA) in 1939, several hundred other fellowships spun off from Alcoholics Anonymous and also incorporated the twelve-step path. The traditions of Alcoholics Anonymous (which many of the other groups have adopted) allow for group autonomy, except on those issues that affect Alcoholics Anonymous as a whole. Thus, you may have one twelve-step recovery group that interprets the twelve steps in an orthodox fashion, and you may have another recovery group that is sensitive to its members talking about other addictions or conditions, such as mental health concerns and trauma (van der Kolk, McFarlane, & Weisaeth, 2007).

Secondly, even though a great number of treatment centers in North America base themselves on the twelve-step philosophy, it is important to remember that these treatment programs are not the voice of Alcoholics Anonymous, Narcotics Anonymous, or any of the other twelve-step groups. It saddens me to hear about individuals who have demeaning, negative experiences at twelve-step-based treatment centers and become scared away from attending twelve-step meetings in the community. I have also seen the reverse happen, where a person in need of treatment can be scared away because of one bad experience with a twelve-step group (or even just a person in that group).

I recognize that there is no such thing as perfect uniformity when it comes to application of twelve-step recovery principles. If anything, there is beauty in that lack of uniformity, especially when it can promote openness in dialogue and understanding, which is something I attempt to do in this book. The mission of this book is to show professionals, twelve-step sponsors, recovering individuals, and family/community members how traditional philosophies like the disease model of addiction and twelve-step recovery can be more competently applied to our work with recovering people by understanding trauma and how it can affect people. I do not claim to represent any particular twelve-step fellowship, and when I reference twelve-step recovery, I am not singling out any fellowship, group, or treatment center specifically. Rather, for the purposes of this book, *twelve-step recovery* refers to the general philosophy of the twelve steps and some of the other slogans and ideas that are typically associated with twelve-step groups (see inset, *Twelve Steps of Alcoholics Anonymous*).

Let's consider what *trauma-sensitive* really means; I tend to use this phrase interchangeably with the phrase *trauma-informed* throughout the book. When we are trauma-sensitive (or trauma-informed), we take into account how traumatic circumstances can shape the human experience—this book, and the strategies suggested within it for building your own personal "trauma toolkits," build upon this idea. There are numerous reasons for recovery communities to embrace this trauma-sensitive approach, the most obvious being that many individuals in addiction recovery affected by trauma return to using drugs or alcohol. If you have spent any time at all working in a treatment center or around twelve-step meetings, this connection is obvious. These individuals often find it difficult to address the past and take appropriate responsibility for their actions while not being overwhelmed by the shame-based ideologies that they acquired as part of their trauma (Hien, Litt, Cohen, Miele, & Campbell, 2009; Miller & Guidry, 2001; Najavits, Weiss, & Shaw, 1997; Ouimette & Newman, 2002).

This trauma can warrant a formal, DSM-IV-TR diagnosis of post-traumatic stress disorder (PTSD), or it can be what Francine Shapiro, founder of Eye Movement Desensitization and Reprocessing (EMDR), referred to as *small-t* trauma. Small-t traumas are disturbances that appear to be at the root of presenting psychopathology. However, small-t traumas are not substantial enough to qualify as a major (i.e., criterion A) trauma, as indicated in the DSM-IV-TR's description of PTSD (American Psychiatric Association, 2000; Maxfield, 2007; Parnell, 2007;

Shapiro & Forrest, 1997; Shapiro, 2001). In Chapter 3, we explore more fully the distinctions between the various types of trauma and exact comorbidity statistics on trauma and addiction. What many of us acknowledge is that, regardless of the type of trauma, its effects can lead to or exacerbate an addictive disorder, and ultimately hinder the recovery process if the trauma is not properly addressed.

Relapse is common in many behavioral disorders, especially addiction (Joseph, Breslin, & Skinner, 1999). Delmonico and Griffin (2007) contended that, in explaining addictive behavior, different models tend to develop over time and independently of each other, even though they are all trying to investigate the causes of addiction and the implications for more effective treatment. Although various models abound to explain relapse, the common theme emerging from the literature is that poor self-efficacy and high volumes of negative emotion, coupled with poor coping skills, put an individual at greatest risk for relapsing on alcohol or other drugs following a period of sobriety (Allsop, Saunders, & Phillips, 2000; Connors & Maisto, 2006; Donovan, 1996; El-Sheikh & Bashir, 2003; Moos & Moos, 2006; Tapert, Ozyurt, Myers, et al., 2004; Walitzer & Dearing, 2006; Walton, Blow, Bingham, et al., 2003). In simpler terms, if you don't like yourself and most of the emotions that you deal with are of the troubling variety, you are going to have a hard time staying sober, *especially* if you haven't learned any meaningful, effective ways to cope.

Miller and Guidry (2001), who developed the Addiction and Trauma Recovery Integration Model (ATRIUM), contended that traditional models of addiction recovery and relapse prevention fail to appropriately consider the significant role that unresolved trauma plays in an addicted individual's attempt at recovery. Miller and Guidry further contended that these traditional approaches tend to marginalize addicted, traumatized women more than their male counterparts. Though Miller and Guidry do not discredit the merit of traditional models such as the twelve-step/Minnesota model of treatment or cognitive-behavioral therapy, they suggest that these approaches do not sufficiently address the role that trauma has played, which can set individuals up to fail in their recovery processes. Though Miller and Guidry's ideas are compatible with common themes on relapse risk factors in the literature (i.e., poor self-efficacy, high volume of negative emotion coupled with poor coping skills), they contend that a more holistic approach to treating addiction is needed to promote long-term recovery and prevent potentially debilitating relapses. This holistic approach means that treatment needs to extend beyond the cognitive interventions that professionals have traditionally used in relapse prevention counseling or the twelve-step oriented methods associated with the Minnesota model.

This book clearly explains how to incorporate a more holistic approach into the addiction recovery process. Regardless of your psychotherapeutic orientation or your personal beliefs about the recovery process, you will benefit from this book. I use the language of twelve-step recovery extensively in this book, which is a reflection of how the majority of treatment programs in the United States operate. However, as your author, I take the position that there are many paths to attaining addiction recovery, as long as the program or selected approach promotes healthy lifestyle change. The imperative that I stress in the book is that regardless of the path chosen to attain recovery, we must take into account the realities of trauma and how to address them.

I use the metaphor of the *toolkit* throughout the book. This metaphor suggests that what you may have learned about recovery before reading this book is not irrelevant. However, by learning an extensive set of trauma-informed skills, you will be able to build on the basics of what you already know about addiction recovery, regardless of your chosen paradigm in approach recovery. If this is your first time reading this book, I encourage you to take few moments and work the toolkit exercises interspersed throughout. Most of these exercises are simple reflections designed to enhance your own critical thinking and self-evaluation about the topics covered in this book. My hope is that, in working these toolkit exercises, you will emerge with a better understanding of how to work twelve-step recovery principles in a manner that is more trauma-sensitive—an understanding that will ultimately help others.

Those of you who do not have much prior experience working with addiction can still benefit, as you will be able to learn how to treat addiction by using your existing theoretical orientation(s) and implementing skills from the trauma toolkit. In chapter 2, "There Is a Solution," I make a case for the implementation of *trauma-sensitive* or *trauma-informed* recovery. Chapter 3 offers readers a simple yet thorough primer on the basics of traumatology. Chapters 4 and 5 look at the pros and cons of twelve-step recovery and other traditional approaches to addiction treatment for an individual affected by trauma. These chapters pay particular attention to the often-slippery fourth- and fifth-step gauntlet. They also emphasize how to apply special considerations when working these steps with traumatized individuals. Chapter 6 highlights the best practices for working with the recovering individual in a manner that is trauma-sensitive, integrating twelve-step principles and the latest knowledge on trauma.

Chapter 7 clearly explains the importance of healthfully using the body as part of trauma-sensitive treatment. Chapter 8 addresses the healing nature of relational elements in the treatment of trauma, and discusses implications for the treatment of addiction. Chapter 9 speaks to the concept of *recovery capital*, or using what a person has going for him to help him build the best recovery program possible. Recovery capital is relevant regardless of theoretical orientation or chosen recovery program, and it is a trauma-sensitive construct that contains multiple implications for enhancing recovery efficacy. Chapter 10 addresses the idea of trauma processing or trauma *reprocessing*. The therapeutic modalities and interventions that people normally associate with "trauma work" (e.g., catharsis-based interventions) are covered in this chapter. Some explanations are given as to what professionals can do with their existing knowledge in this area, and recommendations are given for specialty therapies (and how to make the referrals) that may be useful for addicted individuals struggling with unresolved trauma. The appendix contains quick references of exercises for regulation, containment, and growth that a person can teach himself, or that a clinician or sponsor can use to supplement the benefits of recovery skills in a trauma-sensitive manner.

There is an old, often intoned Chinese proverb to describe trauma and its effects: "Once you've been bitten by a snake, you're afraid even of a piece of coiled rope." Let us remember this wisdom in our work with addicts who affected by trauma, and may we strive to be a healing balm rather than a coiled rope. You will see as you read this book that I am not proposing a reinvention of the wheel, so to speak, when it comes to addiction recovery; however, I attempt to give you the necessary tools to be that healing balm. My challenge for you is to become even more open-minded to the trauma-sensitive perspective in your application of recovery principles when working with others, especially in the twelve-step paradigm. I hope to accomplish this task in as candid of a manner as possible, blending my own stories and ideas together with findings from clinical studies where appropriate. My hope is that, above all, my voice as a recovering individual will come through most strongly, even though I use my professional knowledge to justify the ideas that I put forward in this book.

A Note on Citations

Throughout the book, you will see a series of authors' names and dates following some information. Professional readers will know exactly what these are—APA citations. Casual readers unfamiliar with scholarly writing may ask themselves, "What the heck are those?" Citations let readers know what sources they can look up if they want to check out where the author is getting her information. A reference list at the end of the book contains all of the sources I used to structure many of my arguments. It is good to look at these as "for more information" types of guides if you are not a scholarly reader. Bottom line, don't feel you have to let them bog you down.

A Note on Cases

Unless otherwise indicated, I have changed the names of all cases used in the book to protect anonymity. In many instances, the cases that you are reading are composites (meaning the details of two or more cases are combined) to further guard anonymity.

The Twelve Steps of Alcoholics Anonymous

1. *We admitted we were powerless over alcohol—that our lives had become unmanageable.*

2. *Came to believe that a Power greater than ourselves could restore us to sanity.*

3. *Made a decision to turn our will and our lives over to the care of God as we understood Him.*

4. *Made a searching and fearless moral inventory of ourselves.*

5. *Admitted to God, to ourselves, and to another human being the exact nature of our wrongs.*

6. *Were entirely ready to have God remove all these defects of character.*

7. *Humbly asked Him to remove our shortcomings.*

8. *Made a list of all persons we had harmed, and became willing to make amends to them all.*

9. *Made direct amends to such people wherever possible, except when to do so would injure them or others.*

10. *Continued to take personal inventory and when we were wrong promptly admitted it.*

11. *Sought through prayer and meditation to improve our conscious contact with God as we understood Him, praying only for knowledge of His will for us and the power to carry that out.*

12. *Having had a spiritual awakening as the result of these steps, we tried to carry this message to alcoholics and to practice these principles in all our affairs.*

The Twelve Steps are reprinted with permission of Alcoholics Anonymous World Services, Inc. ("AAWS") Permission to reprint the Twelve Steps does not mean that AAWS has reviewed or approved the contents of this publication, or that AAWS necessarily agrees with the views expressed herein. AA is a program of recovery from alcoholism only—use of the Twelve Steps in connection with programs and activities which are patterned after A.A., but which address other problems, or in any other non-A.A. context, does not imply otherwise.

Toolkit Strategy: Self-Evaluation

Self-evaluation is a skill in and of itself. Knowing where you stand when it comes to your philosophy of working with addicts (and where trauma-sensitivity does or doesn't fit into it) is critical. Take a few minutes to write down how you would describe your approach to working with recovering addicts. You can use the language of psychotherapeutic theory (e.g., twelve-step model, cognitive-behavioral approaches), or you can keep your language informal (e.g., "working a twelve-step program"). Then, consider if there is room in your current approach to take on new, trauma-informed skills. If you have reservations about considering the role of trauma and how it can affect treatment, take a few moments and jot down what your reservations may be about learning these trauma-informed approaches.

CHAPTER 2

There is a Solution

One evening, Nancy showed up at the community drug and alcohol facility in her county with an all-too-familiar feeling. That sense of déjà vu...*I've been here before*. Indeed, her feeling was justified. In the previous twelve years, Nancy had gone through twelve or thirteen treatment facilities (she'd lost count somewhere around five). Additionally, she had participated in AA during and after each treatment episode at the suggestion of each facility, yet she was never able to piece together any more than four months of sobriety. The funny thing was that Nancy never really minded going to AA, she always knew she belonged there. But something just never quite clicked for her.

Nancy sat down with the assessment counselor, still dressed up from an exhausting day of work at a job she hated. There was weariness in her eyes as she explained that the municipal court had sent her for treatment after her third driving under the influence charge. Nancy presented herself in a way that suggested to the counselor that she knew the lingo of twelve-step recovery and treatment. However, Nancy did not need any convincing that she was an alcoholic or an addict.

"Oh, you don't have to diagnose me, I know," she said candidly. "But I can never seem to stay sober, even when I try my hardest."

The assessment counselor, pretty sure that she had established enough rapport with Nancy, began to ask some very tough questions about her history. What emerged from the rest of the interview was the picture of a woman with a complex case of post-traumatic stress disorder (PTSD) due to multiple sexual assaults accompanied by life-threatening violence. Sadly, the perpetrator in many of these assaults was her one-time husband.

"I know that all of this is an issue," Nancy told the counselor, "but I just can't seem to get it all out. And when it comes time for me to do a fourth and fifth step in AA, I just run. I can't look at myself. All I see is garbage—it's too painful, and I run."

Nancy's story is a real-life example of the problem presented in chapter 1. All too often, people labeled as "chronic relapsers" are really just struggling with the aftereffects of unresolved trauma. The legacy of this wounding can last for years, decades even, making tasks like doing a fourth and fifth step (something that is difficult for most addicts) a paralyzing impossibility for the traumatized. This is not to say that a person with unresolved trauma can never do a fourth and fifth step. On the contrary, working all the twelve steps can actually be beneficial for a traumatized person, but only when worked within a safe context that honors the wounds and scars left by the trauma.

Honor the struggle. Sounds like a simple idea, no? Yet in this idea lies a major part of the solution to the dilemma that I outlined in chapter 1. Every time a treatment provider dismisses the impact of a client's history in favor of the "they're just addicts" mentality, he rejects this simple solution. I first heard this phrase, *honor the struggle,* from one of the best bosses I ever had, Mr. Ken Lloyd. The CEO of the community facility where I worked at when I first met Nancy, Mr. Lloyd always stressed the importance of honoring the struggle that our clients experienced before coming to us. Moreover, we were to continue honoring their struggle as they attempted to learn a new way of life in sobriety.

There are those who would argue that placing too much emphasis on a client's history before entering recovery is the kiss of death because a major aspect of twelve-step recovery is to teach an addict to *live in today.* Several major psychotherapeutic schools of thought like reality therapy/ choice theory and rational-emotive behavioral therapy also espouse the importance of living in the now and not dwelling on the past. However, it is important to consider that our histories shape the people we *are* today, and I expound on this concept more fully in chapter 3. So, is there a balance? Can we teach recovering addicts to live *one day at a time* while *honoring the struggle* of their past, present, and future?

I believe there is a balance, and this balance is a key part of the solution. Throughout the 1990s, many books emerged on the market about trauma and addiction interaction, with many of these books presenting models for trauma-informed addiction treatment. Katie Evans and J.

Michael Sullivan (1995) proposed a five-tenet model in their book, *Treating Addicted Survivors of Trauma* that I find especially useful. The five essential components of the Evans-Sullivan model are as follows:

1) A large portion of clients presenting for treatment in any setting have a history of childhood trauma. Respecting this history enhances treatment.

2) Successful treatment of the trauma must include working through memories of the trauma in an experiential way, *after* the clinician and client have established a foundation of safety and coping skills.

3) Substance use disorders are a significant part of the clinical picture for a substantial number of survivors of trauma, thus treatment of the abuse issues that does not address the substance use issues will be ineffective, and treating only the addiction in those with survivor issues will likely be ineffective.

4) The disease model of addiction and conventional twelve-step approaches to treatment are productive in treating the addicted survivor of trauma.

5) Treatment models for addicted survivors of trauma must be *integrated*, and must address the *synergism* of trauma and addiction. A two-track approach is generally ineffective.

I find the five components of the Evans-Sullivan approach to treatment just as relevant today as when they first published them in 1995. The Evans-Sullivan model provides a framework for many of the solutions that I propose in this book.

One of the guiding principles of *Trauma and the Twelve Steps* is that nothing is necessarily wrong with the disease model of addiction, the twelve-step approach to recovery, or other avenues that lead an addicted individual to healthful lifestyle change that promotes recovery. The common denominator that I advocate is that we must respect a person's history of trauma, as Evans and Sullivan purport in the first tenet of their model. Respecting the trauma is commensurate to the idea of honoring the struggle.

The second and third tenets of their model offer an excellent blueprint for conducting treatment in a balanced way. The solution is not to take people in detoxification and make them confront the demons of trauma through hypnosis, and once that is done, they will be free of the addiction! While there are some professionals who believe it is possible to cure a person of his or her addiction by resolving the core trauma that led to the addiction, this approach is far from what I am advocating. Resolving the trauma will not make the addiction go away, just as treating the addiction will not make the effects of the trauma go away. As Evans and Sullivan contend, the trauma must be worked through after a foundation of safety and coping skills have been established. Establishing a modicum of functional sobriety is a part of this safety. However, what frequently happens with recovering people working the twelve steps is that they go into steps four and five—steps that can actually help them with trauma resolution—without having that safe foundation and good coping established first. A recovering person (especially one with trauma issues) needs to be able to regulate, or cope with intense affect or emotional output, before attempting something as daunting as steps four and five.

The fifth element of the Evans-Sullivan model describes my approach to clinical work: the synergism of the trauma and the addiction must be addressed in a manner of treatment that is integrated. This can often lead to rather heated philosophical debates in the manner of *which came first, the chicken or the egg?* In other words, did the trauma lead to the addiction, or did the addiction generate independently of the trauma? Some addiction professionals may be averse to integrated treatment on principle, fearing that it will play into an addict's sense of terminal uniqueness. Other professionals may fear that addressing trauma is stretching the bounds of their job descriptions. "But trauma is out of my league," you may be saying. "I have no experience working with trauma." Although you are not alone in your concerns, I would like to issue a challenge: If you are working with an addicted population, trauma competency is not an option. It is a necessity. Another way to look at the issue: It doesn't matter which came first, the chicken or the egg. What matters is that they are *both* present and they must *both* be addressed.

As Evans and Sullivan state, a large portion of clients presenting for treatment in any setting have a history of childhood trauma. Add to that the trauma of adulthood, or traumas that addicts may have experienced while they were in active addiction, and the picture is further complicated. For instance, if a person was shot while canvassing a neighborhood for drugs, this still qualifies as a trauma. This last statement may puzzle you, especially if you see this shooting as simply a consequence of the person's addiction. However, I hope that chapter 3 will more fully explain for you why a trauma is a trauma is a trauma.

Sound familiar?

Addiction is addiction is addiction…an anthem that rings throughout many treatment centers around the globe.

Same idea.

In this chapter, I introduced you to an approach to trauma-sensitive treatment first published by Evans and Sullivan. This approach, I feel, is a blueprint to the solution. Let's take a closer look at how this approach worked for Nancy, the woman introduced at the beginning of this chapter.

In a follow-up interview that Nancy completed at a later date (Marich, 2009), she shared that simply having the relevance of her trauma acknowledged during the assessment set a positive tone for her treatment episode, and that helped her to feel safe with her counselor. Fortunately,

Nancy was able to stay with the same assessing counselor as her primary counselor for treatment. Nancy was clearly part of the large portion of those who present for treatment with a history of childhood trauma, and her counselor respected this history from the initial assessment (Evans & Sullivan, 1995). During treatment planning, Nancy and her counselor mutually decided that they should directly confront the trauma issues, but only after Nancy established enough of a foundation in her recovery. Thus, the first part of her treatment plan was to complete an eight-week outpatient Twelve-Step Facilitation (Nowiski & Baker, 2003) treatment group, attend three to four AA meetings a week, and begin working the first three steps with a sponsor.

After Nancy completed the Twelve-Step Facilitation treatment group with flying colors, during which time she developed relationships with a sponsor and her support group, she began working with her counselor on coping and relaxation skills, such as deep breathing and guided imagery. Once all of these skills were in place, Nancy agreed that she was ready to directly work on resolving the trauma issues during weekly individual sessions with her counselor at the community treatment center. Nancy's counselor presented her with two possible options: cognitive-behavioral therapy (CBT) and the newer eye movement desensitization and reprocessing (EMDR). Because she heard good things about EMDR at a previous treatment center, Nancy opted to use this therapy to begin the cathartic journey of addressing the multiple abuses that began in preadolescence. Nancy had about three months of continuous sobriety when this journey began, but her counselor proceeded with the work because the foundation of safety and coping skills were in place (Evans & Sullivan, 1995).

After approximately ten weeks of individual sessions, during which time Nancy continued active AA involvement and work with her sponsor on the first three steps, Nancy decided to begin writing out a fourth step. Nancy decided that she wanted her counselor to hear her fifth step. For her, it was important to do a fifth step in an arena where she felt optimally safe. Not only did her counselor create a safe environment in their sessions, but Nancy also felt an extra element of safety because of the counselor's legally binding commitment to confidentiality. Keep in mind, nowhere does it say that the fifth step needs to be heard by a sponsor or a minister, just *another human being* (Alcoholics Anonymous, 2001). Having a fifth step plan that honored her safety gave her some assurance during her fourth-step process, and after resolving a great deal of toxic shame during her EMDR sessions, Nancy was finally able to do a fourth and fifth step.

Nancy continued to work closely with her sponsor, and she continued sessions every other week with her counselor while she worked the rest of the steps. In total, Nancy was involved with the same treatment provider for about a year, staying sober the entire time. Nancy gave her first AA lead upon celebrating eighteen months of sobriety, a remarkable feat considering that she had not previously been able to stay sober any longer than four months. Shortly after this first lead, I interviewed Nancy as part of a follow-up research project, and she shared some amazing insights about her recovery (Marich, 2009). Nancy credited the combination of EMDR, twelve-step work, opening up to a sponsor, seeing addiction as a life-or-death matter, her willing-ness to change, and deepening her spirituality as factors that worked *together* to get her sober and well. She also acknowledged that her trauma history made it difficult for her to work the twelve steps of AA during her prior attempts at recovery:

> *You can't put anything in the proper perspective. And you can't really get a heads up on what really happened because you were so traumatized and you had such bad experiences and, like in my case, I had the trauma then I had the—I call it the after-effect of my ex-husband—pounding over and over and over and over it for like fourteen years after that. I took so much responsibility for it. It was almost like I victimized myself all over again in my mind* (p. 103).

Nancy shared that all of these factors working together helped her achieve a perspective shift that led to her restoration as a sane human being.

Nancy, almost five years sober at the time of this writing, is one of the many profiles in cour-age who have come through the doors of community treatment. Her story is a classic example of someone who benefited from the solution proposed in this book. Consider that this solution began when her counselor honored her struggle during the initial assessment. As the late Fr. Joseph Martin relayed in one of his famous *Chalk Talks*, there really is no place for the "hot seat" in treatment. The point of treatment should be to build up the alcoholic/addict, not tear him down. Although we explore throughout this book how this does not mean letting the addicted person get away with proverbial murder, it is important to honor the humanity of those we work with at all times. Such a simple approach is one of the first steps that we can take to *living in the solution* when it comes to working with traumatized addicts.

Toolkit Strategy: Continued Self-Evaluation

Many professionals have trepidations about working with alcoholics and addicts. However, just as many professionals—even those who are comfortable with treating addiction—seem to have reservations when it comes to addressing trauma as part of an addiction treatment plan. What are your fears or concerns about treating addiction, treating trauma, and especially about treating the two of them together? Common fears that I hear expressed amongst people I teach are "I just don't feel qualified to address the trauma," or "If I get into the trauma stuff too soon, my patient may relapse." Take a few moments to inventory your concerns or potential concerns.

Then, take a look back at the Evans and Sullivan model presented in this chapter. What solutions can you derive from that model that can address your concerns about treating addiction and trauma simultaneously?

CHAPTER 3

Trauma 101

I have to admit, I am sometimes a misfit in the world of social science research and practice. I often attend conferences where my fellow attendees are transfixed by presentations about the latest brain research or the newest meta-analyses with the fanciest research methodologies that prove X, Y, and Z. This is all well and good, and the field needs this...but I remain an English teacher at heart. I actually entered the field of behavioral health as an English teacher. My bachelor's degrees are in American studies (a wing of the English department at the college I attended) and history. My first major job following my graduation was for a Catholic parish in postwar Bosnia-Hercegovina, primarily as an English teacher and language editor. While serving in this capacity, I became blazingly aware of trauma's impact on human development. My pupils were primarily children and young adults who lived at a parish-run children's home. The region was transitioning from decades of a communist-era lifestyle and experiencing the aftermath of a major civil war. Many of my pupils were war orphans, while others had parents who couldn't take care of them simply because of the deplorable social conditions in the country.

An older, American social worker opened my eyes to the reality of traumatic stress and its impact on people. Most noticeably, my students had difficulty focusing. While I witnessed amazing displays of resiliency in these children and young adults, I also witnessed an array of behaviors indicating that many had given up on life. To make a long story short, this experience during the two and a half years I spent in the country impacted me so much that I left my English teaching days behind me, returned to the states, and began a master's degree program in counseling. To bring this back to my original point, even though I now work as a counselor and have no doubt about the validity of my vocation, being an English teacher is still a big part of me. Very often, I am best able to understand complicated clinical phenomena by looking at a word's origin. My approach to the concept of *trauma* is no exception. As with addiction, many models abound for describing and understanding trauma, and this chapter explores several of those models and theories. However, I find the most useful way of explaining the many manifestations of trauma is to go to the word's origin.

The word *trauma* is the Greek word for "wound."

Think for a moment about the word *wound* in a physical sense. What do we know about wounds and the way they heal? When I present live trainings on trauma I ask participants this question because I find that discussing what we know about wounds in the physical sense helps us better understand trauma in the emotional sense. Let's examine some elementary knowledge.

Wounds come in many shapes and sizes. There are open wounds, which include incisions (like from knives), lacerations (tears), abrasions (grazes), punctures, penetration wounds, and the granddaddy of them all, gunshot wounds. Then you have closed wounds, such as contusions (bruises), hematomas (blood tumors), crush injuries, or the slowly forming chronic wounds that can develop from conditions like diabetic ulcers. Each wound has its own distinct character, and various causes can lead to the respective wounding. More importantly, different wounds can affect different people in different ways.

Wow, I used *different* a lot in that last sentence. That's because the word *different* is so important in our discussion of wounding.

Even as I look at the scars from old injuries that are still apparent on my skin, I am amazed at how no two of my wounds look alike. Sure, there are some similar patterns, especially with certain blisters—not to mention scratches from my pets. However, each one has left its distinct imprint on my body. Many of my past wounds have healed quickly, leaving no sign of physical scarring at all, whereas others have healed without complication but have left a mark, a reminder. And what I've mused on so far in this paragraph just applies to me!

One of the miracles of creation is that no two people are alike. Add this idea to the reality of wounding, and we see that even if I experience an injury similar to yours, it is quite unlikely that we will wound in exactly the same way. Furthermore, even though wound healing follows a similar process in human beings, a myriad of other variables complicates the process. As an example, if one person experiences a laceration as a result of a sporting accident but her white blood cell production is poor and her overall Vitamin C levels are low, it is likely she will take longer to heal than her peer with better white blood cell production and higher Vitamin C levels who experiences the same injury. These are just two examples of possible variables that can affect physical healing. Think about other factors like age, health conditions, overall skin plasticity, genetic disorders (e.g., hemophilia), location of the wound, and how soon the patient received appropriate treatment.

Most will agree that failure to receive the proper treatment after a wounding can complicate the healing process. Sure, some wounds, especially minor ones, often clear up on their own with little or no treatment. Consider the difference between a healthy man experiencing a minor scrape and a hemophiliac getting that same scrape. Treatment could be a life or death matter for the hemophiliac because of his condition. Most wounds require some level of treatment, even if that treatment is as simple as cleaning the wound and putting a bandage or anti-bacterial cream on it. Significant wounds may need sutures or stitches accompanied by a dose of precautionary antibiotics. The most severe wounds—stabs or gunshot wounds— require immediate medical attention, or the sufferer risks loss of a limb in the long term (especially if infection sets in). Death can result in the worst cases. In sum, if the injured neglects requisite treatment, the wound can get worse, and this worsening can lead to other debilitating physical symptoms.

When wounds don't receive the proper treatment, there is a great chance that complications will result from the wound worsening. What if the wound never gets a chance to heal because outside forces keep picking at the wound? This question is a no-brainer for most people. We know that if wounds don't receive treatment but instead become further assaulted (e.g., the old cliché, *salting the wound*), then the wounds are going to get worse, which will delay healing. If this concept makes sense to you when it comes to physical wounds, my challenge for you is to apply this same knowledge to emotional trauma.

Like physical wounds, emotional traumas come in various shapes and sizes for people, resulting from a variety of causes. For some people, simple traumas (wounds) can clear up on their own, but for others with more complicating emotional variables (many of which can be biologically based), the healing process may take longer. If an individual who has experienced a major emotional trauma doesn't obtain the proper conditions to heal (which can include formal mental health treatment) it will likely take longer for the trauma to clear up, and it could end up causing other symptoms. A major factor when drawing parallels between physical and emotional trauma is the notion of rewounding. If a person experiences a traumatic event and does not receive the optimal conditions in which to heal, that is bad enough. But then imagine if other people in his life keep picking at the wound with their insensitive comments and potentially retraumatizing behaviors. Of course, the wound is never going to get better, or, in all likelihood, it will worsen.

Let's look at a specific example here using one of the classic sayings from the addiction treatment field: *The three unwritten rules of an alcoholic home are don't talk, don't trust, and don't feel.* These three conditions, as we will examine throughout the book, create the perfect environment for emotional wounds to fester. It's like putting a person with an open physical sore in a tank of bacteria. So imagine that a child in an alcoholic home gets teased mercilessly by bullies at school, perhaps in situations where she genuinely feels her life is endangered. That situation in and of itself would qualify as a trauma. Then, the little girl comes home and her father tells her to just put up and shut up. She receives no help or consolation for the emotional wounding that she's been experiencing at school. Moreover, the names that her father calls her, especially when he is drunk, simply reinforce what the bullies are making her feel about herself. Thus, her wound never gets a chance to heal. Not only that, but the wound worsens when she goes home.

Many definitions and models in the field explain trauma. I want to challenge you to think about the parallels between physical and emotional wounds because it is my belief that this is one of the simplest ways to understand trauma and *how it affects different people in different ways.* I am still saddened when I hear stories of therapists minimizing a person's trauma because he may not have had it as bad as someone else in the same treatment group may have, or he may not have suffered as badly as another client did. *If it is traumatic for the client, then it is traumatic; it is worthy of addressing clinically.* I have embraced this axiom since the very beginning of my career, and I believe that it has helped to promote positive, healing relationships with my clients. I am glad that people who worked with me in therapy over the years adopted this approach with me, or I may have denied myself the treatment and wound care that I needed. All too often, I hear clients say, "Well, that really wasn't a trauma, it's not like I went to war or I was raped or anything…."

Sound like something you may have heard before?

Let's examine how some of these old ideas about trauma being synonymous with PTSD, and the "big traumas" like war and rape are not optimal. The PTSD diagnosis first appeared in DSM-III in 1980, following a series of political advocacy maneuvers related to the Vietnam War. It had become clear to the psychotherapeutic professions that wars profoundly impacted many of those who fought them, and after the PTSD diagnosis premiered, it was obvious that survivors of other life-threatening events, such as violent crimes, natural disasters, and major accidents, exhibited similar symptoms. According to the DSM-IV-TR (American Psychiatric Association, 2000), for PTSD to be officially diagnosed, the individual must have experienced a Criterion A trauma. By definition, a Criterion A trauma is experiencing or witnessing an event that is life threatening or is perceived to be life threatening, resulting in a response of helplessness or horror.

Many clinicians do not think to look further, and in doing assessments, if they do not hear that a major trauma has taken place (like a fire or war combat) they do not pursue the issue of trauma further. I always challenge those I train to look deeper, just within the PTSD diagnosis; you may be surprised at what you find. Remember, a Criterion A trauma can be *perceived* as life threatening, and it can still qualify. This allows us to honor the subjective nature of trauma. Think about a five-year-old child growing up in an alcoholic home, routinely watching his alcoholic father beating his alcoholic mother. If that child perceives that his mother's life is in danger and his life may be next, it would qualify as a Criterion A trauma. Once again, it is a subjective experience. Another child in the same family may not perceive these events as life threatening, just very stressful. This is why, in conducting assessments, it is important that we get a sense of what these traumatic or wounding experiences *meant* to a client.

If you look a little further into the PTSD diagnosis as it appears in the DSM-IV-TR (the diagnostic manual of mental and emotional disorders used by clinical professionals), there is even more revealing information that many clinicians do not even realize is there. I like to call this quick list my "nutshell" definition of PTSD:

Actual or perceived threat of injury or death—response of hopelessness or horror (Criterion A)

<u>Re-experiencing</u> of the trauma (Criterion B)

<u>Avoidance</u> of stimuli associated with the trauma (Criterion C)

<u>Heightened arousal</u> symptoms (Criterion D)

Duration of symptoms longer than 1 month

Functional impairment due to disturbances

Let's take a closer look at Criterion B, C, and D, and I will share with you my experiences regarding what clinicians tend to overlook when it comes to trauma. Keep in mind that even though some slight modifications will appear in the PTSD diagnosis of DSM-5 (scheduled for release in the next year), we can still use the existing criteria in the DSM-IV-TR as teaching points in this chapter.

Criterion B covers those symptoms that mark a reexperiencing of the trauma. The classic examples of reexperiencing symptoms are flashbacks, vivid dreams, and nightmares. However, what many people do not realize is that hallucinations can also be a part of Criterion B experiences. I remember a case that a colleague of mine once treated. This man, who we'll call Jim, was a severe cocaine addict with a wide spectrum of mental health symptoms, including hallucinations. Jim, who had intermittent sobriety over the years, was nonresponsive to just about any medication he took for his hallucinatory symptoms. My colleague was wise enough to explore the content of his auditory hallucinations further, and it turns out that the "voice" telling him to kill himself was his abusive father. I truly believe that my colleague's ability to identify the root cause of his voices helped to enhance Jim's overall treatment experience, and when I last heard about his progress, he had more than four years of sobriety. My main message here is this: when a client talks about hearing or seeing things, don't automatically wash your hands of it and defer these symptoms to a psychiatrist.

Ask.

Ask about the content of the voices and how they may be a part of the client's larger history. You may find out that getting these issues out on the table will enhance the treatment experience.

Criterion C refers to avoidance of stimuli associated with the trauma. The major symptoms that clinicians associate with this criterion include the person steering away from reminders of the trauma, such as not driving near the site of a crime or not wanting to talk about anything connected to the trauma. However, there are many more potential manifestations of Criterion C, including isolation, withdrawal from activities that used to be important, having a sense of a foreshortened future, restrictive range of affect, and fear of feelings. There are some clear parallels here to substance-use disorders. First, when an individual has a sense of a foreshortened future, instant gratification becomes more appealing (Fletcher, 1996; Terr, 1991). Second, if a person is afraid of feeling or showing emotion related to traumatic etiology, drugs and/or alcohol may become a very appealing aid to keeping those feelings suppressed. Although Criterion C does not directly mention substances, the parallel is clear.

Consider the case of a girl we'll call Rachel. An uncle sexually abused her during her elementary school years, and she was never able to tell anybody. Although the abuse stopped by the time she was eight, during her teenage years and early adulthood, her family required her to go to holiday gatherings at her grandmother's house, where she had to see her uncle. Sometimes, she felt forced into the position of making small talk with him. After Rachel tried marijuana for the first time at the age of fourteen, she surmised that if she had to go to these happy family gatherings, smoking a joint before she went (and after she returned) helped her not to feel the overwhelming sense of anxiety that emerged from having contact with her abuser. These experiences with smoking a joint to avoid the pain crystallized with her. She adopted this strategy into her adult life for dealing with uncomfortable emotions.

Many traumatized individuals have also called upon drugs and alcohol for dealing with symptoms associated with Criterion D, heightened arousal symptoms. The two major symptoms we associate with this category are hypervigilance (e.g., always being on guard for something bad to happen) and an exaggerated startle response (in which a person is more "jumpy" than what would be considered normal). However, clinicians tend to overlook the fact that three other major avoidance symptoms often get lumped into other diagnostic categories without ever examining the trauma. One of the listed symptoms in DSM-IV-TR that can fall under Criterion D is problems focusing or paying attention. However, when people come into treatment (either addiction or mental health), clinicians often attribute such a symptom to attention-deficit disorder. Sleep disturbance, which includes problems falling or staying asleep (without nightmares), is a valid symptom under Criterion D. Yet how many times are people with sleeping difficulties simply put on a medication without clinicians exploring the root issues? Other possible symptoms listed under Criterion D are increased irritability and outbursts of anger. Yet when many clients present with these symptoms, I have often seen one of two things happen. Mental health traditionalists often lump these symptoms into the bipolar spectrum, and addiction traditionalists write these symptoms off as part of the addiction. Once again, does the trauma better explain these symptoms? These are the questions we need to ask and critically evaluate.

Now, please don't get me wrong. I'm not discounting the existence of attention-deficit or bipolar disorders, nor am I refuting the notion that a person's anger difficulties can be a part of their addiction manifestation. I am simply challenging professionals to look deeper because it can enhance the treatment process if we do. It's important to explore whether trauma better explains some symptoms people demonstrate at our treatment centers, be it diagnosable PTSD per the DSM-IV-TR or other clinically significant trauma.

In this next section, we consider how trauma does not necessarily need to be Criterion A for it to be clinically significant. This is where many clients get tripped up, believing that if they didn't survive a major disaster, then their trauma is somehow less legitimate. As noted earlier, I have sadly seen many professionals and family members further reinforce this devastating belief. A useful concept for helping us to further understand the idea of trauma that does not meet criteria for PTSD comes from Dr. Francine Shapiro, founder of EMDR. Dr. Shapiro introduced the notion of small-t trauma. Small-t traumas are the upsetting events that life sends our way (Shapiro & Forrest, 1997); however, if these small-t traumas are not resolved, or processed, then we can stay stuck in this disturbance. Let's look at a case to better explain this idea.

Jane entered treatment for crack cocaine addiction in her early forties. Even though she had a series of Criterion A traumas throughout her childhood, she reported that the first time she ever remembered feeling like she was worthless and not good enough was during the first grade. Jane indicated that she had a very small bladder (a condition that was later verified medically), and as a result, she required frequent trips to the restroom. One day in the first grade, Jane asked her teacher if she could go to the bathroom, and the teacher flatly refused. Jane continued to plead, but to no avail. After several minutes, Jane was no longer able to physically hold it (despite her best efforts), and she urinated right there at her seat, which got her into further trouble with her teacher. Jane became the butt of her peers' cruel taunts, and it became an experience she was never able to live down throughout her school years. Yet as I treated Jane, she told me this story with a great deal of shame, crying the deep, profound tears that we may expect to see from someone who had experienced physical assault. Clearly, Jane experienced assault at the level of her psyche, and because she was never able to talk about or make sense of the experience, she stayed stuck in the message that the experience gave her: *Jane, you are worthless and not good enough. You can't even wait to go to the bathroom.*

It is amazing how these experiences that may seem minor or silly on the surface can cause profound scarring, especially if our brains, which are hardwired for adaptive resolution of input, are not able to make sense of the wounding (Grey, 2008; Shapiro, 2001; Shapiro & Solomon, 2008). For Jane, those early messages of "I am worthless" and "I'm not good enough" stayed in her brain like file folders through which all other life experiences filtered. The table that appears at the end of this chapter is a list of the "greatest hits" of negative cognitions that others and I have most frequently encountered in working with traumatized individuals.

Like Jane, I think we may all have these small-t stories somewhere in our past, each of them wounding us in their own distinct way. I know that when I went through treatment, there were two major small-t incidents that I needed to address. The first was when I was five years old and my pediatrician called me a "fatso." The other was when a boy at the Catholic school I attended made me think that he liked me. When I agreed to "go out" with him (as much as sixth graders can go out, mind you), he (and several of the other popular girls who had put him up to it) laughed in my face and called me pathetic. Indeed, both experiences solidified my own negative beliefs that I was ugly and pathetic; I needed to address both experiences clinically later in my life, and I am glad that I did.

After one of my lectures, in which I explained the concept of small-t trauma, a professional man wearing a smart three-piece business suit came up to me and sheepishly admitted, "I'm afraid of cafeterias, and I think I know why." He admitted that when he was in elementary school, he dropped his tray full of food in the cafeteria in front of what seemed like the entire student body. The children laughed at him mercilessly, and the school required him to clean up the mess in front of everyone as they taunted him and called him names. Because the man was never able to process or make sense of the experience, it stayed stuck in his psyche. As he told me, he avoids cafeterias like the plague, even the one at his place of business.

What is interesting about Jane's story, my story, and the businessman's story is that all of these events happened when we were in elementary school—in our formative years, so to speak. Let's set a broader context for these experiences. In his stages of psychosocial development, Erikson (1950, 1959) identified the elementary school years (between ages seven and twelve) as the prime time for the development of self-confidence. In this elementary school stage (industry versus inferiority), if children are ridiculed and punished for their efforts (as opposed to praised and encouraged, especially by adult figures), feelings and beliefs of inferiority can develop. As Alfred Adler contended, an individual's essential lifestyle patterns form in childhood as a way to cope with any feelings and beliefs of inferiority that emerge (Adler, 1931; Mozak, 2000). Adler first introduced the concept of the "life style" as the pair of glasses through which an individual sees the world, glasses that we have designed to deal with our feelings of inferiority. I expound upon this Adlerian concept in chapters 4 and 6 in describing the best practices for trauma-sensitive treatment. Few will argue that lifestyle change is a critical component for successful addiction recovery, and trauma-sensitive approaches can give us (as professionals and sponsors) a better idea of where, when, and how faulty lifestyle patterns first developed.

Some of you may be shaking your heads in overwhelming agreement. This may upset others of you who are saying something like, "Okay, so you wet your pants in front of everyone when you were six years old, get over it already." Although few people would argue that *getting over it* is the optimal task to accomplish for wellness, getting over it may not be as easy for some as it is for others. We discuss the importance of the formative elementary school years in this chapter. In addition we can take this discussion back even deeper to instances of birth trauma (e.g., breech births, losing a twin in childbirth) and perinatal trauma (e.g., being in utero when the mother has a major, traumatic experience, having a mother who drinks, smokes, or does drugs during gestation) and how those can shape the human experience (Grof, 1991). Many individuals who are having a tough time getting over trauma can likely trace their traumatic experiences back to preverbal origins. The rest of this chapter puts the idea of trauma's impact across the lifespan into further view as we consider what various disciplines have published about trauma and how this knowledge can help us better address the tough question of why getting over traumas can be so hard to do.

Biologically speaking, when we ask a person to just *think it through*, or *leave it in the past*, we may be asking a person to do something that is neurologically impossible for them. The best way that I know how to explain this phenomenon is to turn to MacLean's (1990) notion of the triune brain. The triune brain model acknowledges that the human brain really operates as three separate brains, each with their own special roles, which include respective senses of time, space, and memory. The three regions of the whole brain include:

- The R-Complex Brain (Reptilian Brain): includes the brain stem and cerebellum; controls instinctual survival behaviors, muscle control, balance, breathing, and heartbeat. The reptilian brain is very reactive to direct stimuli.

- The Limbic Brain: contains the amygdala, hypothalamus, and hippocampus. The limbic system is the source of emotions and instincts within the brain, responsible for the five

*F*s: flight, fight, freeze, feed, and sexual behavior (fill in the *F* blank on that one). When something activates this part of the brain, it activates emotion. According to MacLean, everything in the limbic system is either agreeable (pleasure) or disagreeable (pain), and that survival is based on the avoidance of pain and the reoccurrence of pleasure.

• The Neocortex (or Cerebral Cortex): is unique to mammals. It is this higher region of the brain that regulates our executive functioning, which can include higher-order thinking skills, reason, speech, and sapience (e.g., wisdom, calling upon experience). The limbic system needs to interact with the neocortex to process emotions.

In essence, when we encourage recovering people to put their intellect (I) over their emotions (E), we are asking them to use their neocortex. You may have heard the slogan "I/E, not E/I" in certain twelve-step recovery forums.

Many twelve-step strategies and cognitive therapies activate and work with the neocortex, yet for a person with unprocessed trauma symptoms, the three regions of the brain are not optimally communicating with each other. Indeed, during periods of intense emotional disturbance, a human being cannot optimally access the functions of the neocortex because the limbic, or emotional brain, is in control (Solomon & Siegel, 2003; Van Der Kolk, 2003). This is why the visceral experience of triggers—be they triggers to use an addictive substance or triggers for traumatic symptoms to surface—are limbic-level activities that cannot be easily addressed using neocortical functions. Moreover, if something triggers a person into a fight, flight, or freeze response at the limbic level, one of the quickest ways to alleviate that pain is to feed the pleasure potential in the limbic system. As many traumatized addicts have discovered, alcohol use, drug use, food, sex, or other reinforcing activities are particularly effective at killing the pain.

One way that traumatized people operate is to become "stuck in limbic." The limbic region of the brain activates during the original trauma to help the traumatized person survive (through flight, fight, or freeze), but for a variety of reasons, they are never able to link up that limbic activation to the neocortex. As indicated in the triune brain model, linking the limbic brain with the neocortical brain is requisite for processing, or making sense of, these troubling emotions and reconsolidating them into their human experience.

Author Lily Burana (2009), who is not a professional clinician but who has survived her own battle with PTSD, explains what happens in the brain of a traumatized person better than any psychotherapeutic professional I have ever encountered. I like her explanation best of all because it elucidates a complex scientific phenomenon in lay language:

> PTSD means, in "talking over beer" terms, that you've got some crossed
> wires in your brain due to the traumatic event. The overload of stress makes

your panic button touchier than most people's, so certain things trigger a stress reaction—or more candidly—an over-reaction. Sometimes, the panic button gets stuck altogether and you're in a state of constant alert, buzzing and twitchy and aggressive. Your amygdala—the instinctive flight, fight, or freeze part of your brain—reacts to a trigger before your rational mind can deter it. You can tell yourself, "it's okay," but your wily brain is already ten steps ahead of the game, registering danger and sounding the alarm. So you might say once again, in a calm, reasoned cognitive-behavioral-therapy kind of way, "Brain, it's okay." But your brain yells back, "Bullshit kid, how dumb do you think I am? I'm not falling for that one again." By then, you're hiding in the closet, hiding in a bottle, and/or hiding from life, crying, raging, or ignoring the phone and watching the counter on the answering machine go up, up, up, and up. You can't relax, and you can't concentrate because the demons are still pulling at your strings. The long-range result is that the peace of mind you deserve in the present is held hostage by the terror of your past (pp. 226–227).

I have heard and read all of the famous trauma scholars in the field throughout my training, and I have never heard anyone express the complex biopsychosocial-spiritual effects of trauma so succinctly and eloquently. I challenge you to reread Lily Burana's explanation and ask yourself if it sounds like any of the traumatized addicts you have treated or worked with in twelve-step recovery communities.

Of course, the information I have presented to you about trauma is not without controversy (Golden & Bergo, 2009), some even go as far as calling the potential aftereffects of trauma a myth (Clancy, 2010). Another major criticism is that people often use the diagnosis of PTSD, like addiction, to explain away unacceptable behavior (e.g., he beat his wife up after returning from Iraq because of his PTSD). One reason people often struggle to wrap their understanding around trauma's impact on functioning is because the horrible aftereffects do not happen to everybody. Indeed, many individuals who experience horrific traumas do not go on to develop PTSD or other problems in functioning. The simplest way that I can explain this is to once again refer you to the wound parallel from the beginning of this chapter. No two people wound in the exact same way, and the conditions that exist immediately after the wounding can have a significant impact on how a person will heal (and deal) with the wound long term. Trauma expert Bessel van der Kolk (2003) contended that many variables play a role in determining how trauma will affect a person long term, including the severity of the original trauma, the severity/intensity of the initial trauma-related symptoms, the age at which the trauma occurred, the length of time that the trauma lasted, and the degree of positive social-cultural support that surrounded the individual at the time of the trauma. Van der Kolk, citing a century of evidence from psychological research, also noted that the cognitive or intellectual ability to comprehend a traumatic experience might also play a critical role in making an experience that may simply be stressful to one person traumatic to another.

Processing is a term associated with the discussion of trauma. Processing is really just a fancy psychological term for making sense of an experience, or as van der Kolk calls it, comprehending a traumatic experience. Processing is a way to achieve the resolution needed to move on from a traumatic experience or series of experiences. Some have even called processing the *digesting* of an unsettling event. If we are using the wound parallel, processing occurs when the wound receives proper treatment within an appropriate time frame, and we allow the individual space to heal. In a biological sense, referring once again to MacLean's (1990) triune brain model, processing occurs when the emotional material in the limbic brain can link up with the more rationally oriented functions in the neocortical brain.

There are a variety of reasons that trauma remains unprocessed, undigested, unresolved, or unhealed (pick whichever word makes the most sense to you). I explained one of the major reasons earlier in the chapter when I asked you to consider a girl who grew up in an alcoholic home while kids at school bullied her. The entire *don't talk, don't trust, don't feel* culture of that home is completely antithetical to the notion of processing, making it easy for the traumatic memories to stay stuck in limbic. Another reason trauma remains unprocessed is because people tend to automatically assume that talking is the only way a person can process. In fact, in many treatment centers (both addiction and mental health), talking is synonymous with processing. Although talking can help a person to process, it is primarily a function of the neocortical brain. A person can talk about the trauma all they want, but until they can address it at the limbic level, the trauma may stay stuck.

Other healthy modalities of processing can include exercise, breath work, imagery, journaling, drawing, or prayer. The physical act of picking up the phone to call your sponsor can be a form of processing (because you are using the body for a healthy, adaptive purpose), even if no one is available to talk to you on the other line. Addictive substances and behaviors can be a traumatized person's attempt to address the pain that is blaring in their limbic system, and they find it so effective because these substances and behaviors can seem so pleasurable to the body. Our challenge is to help traumatized addicts use their bodies in healthier ways that promote adaptive processing of information. Chapter 7 explores in depth why these body-based activities can actually be some of the most effective mechanisms for processing, digesting, resolving, or healing trauma.

If you have worked with addicts for any length of time, the links between trauma and addiction ought to have manifested themselves to you already. It is hard to pinpoint exact numbers about the prevalence of comorbidity between trauma and addiction for several reasons. First, as noted by Briere and Scott (2006), the term *trauma* really only refers to the wounding event itself: the effects of the trauma can be multifarious, ranging from diagnosable PTSD as defined by the DSM-IV-TR to instances of depression or panic symptoms that may result from small-t traumas. Thus, respective studies may define trauma-related sequelae in different fashions. Nomenclature always makes comparing studies interesting due to the differences in operational definitions and inconsistent use of constructs amongst the studies (e.g., addictive disorders versus substance dependence versus substance use disorders, which can include both abuse and dependence). Additionally, the inaccuracy in client (or study participant) reporting due to memory gaps or fear of stigmatization may also be a factor in some of the disparity in the numbers. Taking all of that into consideration, here are some numbers and connections that researchers gathered about the nature of the problem:

✓ There is high comorbidity between PTSD and substance use disorders: 27.9 percent of those with PTSD meet criteria for substance abuse, and an additional 34.5 percent meet criteria for dependence (Kessler, Sonnega, Bromet, Hughes & Nelson, 1995).

✓ Various studies (Abueg & Fairbank, 1992; Chilicoat & Breslau, 1998; Fullilove et al., 1993; Hernandez & DiClemente, 1992; Keane & Wolf, 1990; Kulka et al., 1990; Lisak, 1993) have found a disproportionately higher percentage of abuse, neglect, or trauma histories in substance abusers than in the general population.

✓ Of patients in substance disorder treatment, 12 to 34 percent have PTSD; these numbers can be as high as 33 to 59 percent in women (Najavits, 2001; 2006).

✓ In a snapshot study conducted by Fullilove et al. in 1993, 59 percent of patients at an inpatient, drug rehab center met criteria for PTSD.

✓ Brown and Gilman (2008) reported that amongst those who met criteria for a county drug court that they studied, 65 percent of those eligible participants were affected by trauma in some way: 26 percent met criteria for PTSD, 35 percent reported some PTSD symptoms connected to a trauma but did not meet full criteria for PTSD as defined by the DSM, and 3.9 percent had experienced a Criterion A trauma at some point in their life but had no experience of PTSD symptoms.

✔ Individuals with a history of PTSD were more likely to have a history of many other psychiatric disorders, an increased risk for alcohol dependence, and other significant psychosocial impairments (Peirce, Kindbom, Waesche, Yuscavage & Brooner, 2008).

✔ Substance abuse increases the likelihood of victimization (Cottler, Compton, Mager, Spitznagel & Janca, 1992; Hien, Litt, Cohen, Miele & Campbell, 2009; Resnick, Yehuda & Acierno, 1997; Ursano et al., 1999), which can further promulgate the vicious cycle of coping with trauma-related stress and self-medicating with addictive substances (Briere & Scott, 2006).

Given all of these numbers, it is clear why substance abuse in and of itself is identified as a potential trauma-related response in individuals with both PTSD and complex PTSD or disorders of extreme stress, not otherwise specified (DESNOS) (Courtis & Ford, 2009; Najavits, 2001; Ouimette & Brown, 2002).

Classics to Check Out

Because this book is not meant to be primarily academic, I have elected not to go into an extensive "literature review" of everything that's out there on the subject of trauma or integrated trauma and addiction treatment. Much of what I cite in this book is simply the ideas that I have found most useful in my clinical development, but my citations are not exhaustive. Here is a list of popular, clinical resources that you might try if you are looking to expand your knowledge base in the area of trauma and addiction interaction even further:

Courtis, C. A., & Ford, J. D. (2009). *Treating complex traumatic stress disorders: An evidence-based guide.* New York: The Guilford Press.

Dayton, T. (2000). *Trauma and addiction: Ending the cycle of pain through emotional literacy.* Deerfield Beach, FL: Health Communications, Inc.

Duncan, B. L., Miller, S. D., Wampold, B. E., & Hubble, M. A. (Eds.) (2009). *The heart and soul of change: Delivering what works in therapy.* 2nd ed. Washington, D. C.: American Psychological Association.

Grey, E. (2010). *Unify your mind: Connecting the feelers, thinkers, & doers of your brain.* Pittsburgh, PA: CMH&W, Inc.

Herman, J. L. (1992). *Trauma and recovery.* New York: Basic Books.

Hien, D., Litt, L. C., Cohen, L. R., Miele, G. M., & Campbell, A. (2009). *Trauma services for women in substance abuse treatment: An integrated approach.* Washington, DC: American Psychological Association Press.

Levine, P. (1997). *Waking the tiger—Healing trauma.* Berkeley, CA: North Atlantic Books.

MacLean, P. D. (1990). *The triune brain in evolution: Role in paleocerebral functions.* New York: Plenum Press.

Miller, D. & Guidry, L. (2001). *Addictions and trauma recovery: Healing the body, mind, and spirit.* New York: W.W. Norton.

Najavits, L. (2001). *Seeking safety: A treatment manual for PTSD and substance abuse.* New York: The Guilford Press.

Ouimette, P., & Brown, P. J. (2002). *Trauma and substance abuse: Causes, consequences, and treatment of comorbid disorders.* Washington, DC: American Psychological Association Press.

Rothschild, B. (2000). *The body remembers: The psychophysiology of trauma treatment.* New York: W. W. Norton & Company.

Scaer, R. (2005). *The trauma spectrum: Hidden wounds and human resiliency.* New York: W. W. Norton & Company.

Solomon, M. F., & Siegel, D. (2003). *Healing trauma: Attachment, mind, body, and brain.* New York: W. W. Norton & Company.

van der Kolk, B., McFarlane, A., & Weisaeth, L. (Eds.). (1996). *Traumatic stress: The effects of overwhelming experience on mind, body, and society.* New York: The Guilford Press.

You may also consider checking out the Sanctuary Model ®, a crystallization of Dr. Sandra Bloom's work at www.sanctuaryweb.com. Several other excellent, trademarked models and approaches are available in the addiction community that can that can blend well with the approaches proposed in *Trauma and the Twelve Steps*.

Complex PTSD

I cannot write a chapter on the basics of trauma without addressing complex PTSD (otherwise known as disorders of extreme stress, not otherwise specified, or DESNOS), a phenomenon that has received a great deal of attention since Judith Herman first published the concept in 1992. DESNOS is currently under review for the forthcoming DSM-5, as are some modifications to the existing PTSD diagnosis (American Psychiatric Association, 2010). Although not an official DSM-IV-TR diagnosis, the notion of complex traumatic stress disorders seems all too familiar to many clinicians. Complex PTSD respects the idea that original wounds, or traumas, can become further complicated due to a variety of conditions. Courtis and Ford (2009; p.1) identify these conditions as traumatic stressors that meet the following conditions:

- Are repetitive or prolonged

- Involve direct harm and/or neglect or abandonment by caregivers or ostensibly responsible adults

- Occur at developmentally vulnerable times in the victim's life, such as early childhood

- Have great potential to severely compromise a child's development

Essentially, it is a given that trauma can seriously affect someone's life. But have you ever met a person who has grown up in a culture of trauma? Have you ever dealt with a person who has so many wounds all over their psyche that you are really baffled as to where to begin the healing process? Have you ever met a client (or a newcomer to a twelve-step program) who, when you ask her if she has experienced any trauma in her life says, "Where do I even begin?" If so, you have probably encountered complex trauma.

Demystifying Dissociation

In learning about the basics of trauma and how to address it, covering the concept of dissociation is imperative. Although dissociative disorders technically have their own diagnostic classifications in the DSM-IV-TR, I do not believe I have ever treated a client for one of the dissociative disorders without uncovering a major trauma warranting a formal PTSD diagnosis. On the flipside, it is common for individuals with a PTSD diagnosis to experience symptoms of dissociation without an official dissociative disorder diagnosis being present. This makes sense considering that dissociative flashback is one of the potential reexperiencing symptoms (Criterion B) that an individual may endure as part of a PTSD diagnosis.

Dissociation and trauma-related disorders are interrelated because dissociation is an extreme defense that the mind can call upon to handle intense disturbance. The most extreme forms of dissociation, such as dissociative identity disorder (DID, formerly known as multiple personality disorder), dissociative amnesia, and dissociative fugue can stump even the most seasoned professionals. However, professionals can address even these often-baffling disorders using some of the principles covered in this book and a sense of open-mindedness. As one of my more memorable clients with DID shared with me many years ago, "People fear what they don't understand." In the spirit of his astute observation, I have learned that one of the first steps we, as professionals, can take to overcome dissociation is to deal with our own fears and concerns about people who dissociate.

The sheer reality is that, at one time or another, we have all dissociated. If you've ever daydreamed, you've dissociated. If you've ever wished with every fiber in your being that you were somewhere else other than where you were—and the wish became so intense you actually brought another place into view—you've dissociated. If you've ever "zoned out" and stopped listening to someone speak because you were either intensely bored or intensely disturbed, then you have dissociated. If you've ever done a "calm place" visualization exercise or guided imagery, you have dissociated in a therapeutic way! It's just that people who warrant a formal diagnosis of dissociative disorder, or people who experience dissociation as part of their PTSD, do it so much or so intensely as a way to assuage the pain of disturbing stimuli that it causes functional impairment.

A useful passage that demystifies dissociation comes from Elizabeth Howell (2008), author of *The Dissociative Mind*:

> The rising tide of trauma and dissociation studies has created a sea change in the way we think about psychopathology. Chronic trauma…that occurs early in life has profound effects on personality development and can lead to the development of dissociative identity disorder (DID), other dissociative disorders, personality disorders, psychotic thinking, and a host of symptoms such as anxiety, depression, eating disorders, and substance abuse. In my view, DID is simply an extreme version of the dissociative structure of the psyche that characterizes us all. Dissociation, in a general sense, refers to the rigid separation of parts of experience, including somatic experience, consciousness, affects, perception, identity, and memory.

Howell's book was essential reading early in my career to help me overcome my fears and concerns about working with dissociation in a professional context, and I strongly recommend it to all professionals working with trauma and addiction. My client's comment about people fearing what they do not understand certainly spawned this inquiry within me.

The first step is overcoming your personal fears about encountering dissociation when you see it: Remember, the types of dissociation that tend to freak professionals out in sessions or in groups is simply extreme, maladaptive coping. Having an arsenal of multisensory grounding and stabilization skills at the ready is the simplest solution. Teaching clients prone to dissociation these skills ahead of time is vital to helping them if their dissociation becomes problematic or impairing. We thoroughly review the multisensory skills in later chapters. As I teach certain skills throughout the book, I indicate which skills tend to be best for those who struggle with dissociation, and I provide some cautions about which skills may need to be adapted for those who are prone to dissociating.

Understanding dissociation takes on a new level of importance as we discuss addiction treatment for one simple reason: groups. Yes, dissociation is a potential issue in individual therapy, with all addicted clients struggling with trauma, but the complexities of group work and twelve-step or other recovery meetings can trigger dissociative responses in individuals. Think about it critically: A client may be sitting in group just listening to someone else share, and the other group member may say something that triggers an emotional response within the client—a response that she may not be ready to deal with. Odds are, when someone is "zoning out" in groups or in a meeting, this is exactly what is happening. Although there are many benefits to treatment groups and recovery meetings, dissociation is a great risk for traumatized individuals who are early on in their recovery process. If you are a group facilitator, acknowledging this risk is important, and making yourself available individually after a group meeting to meet with someone who has dissociated is vital. Another preventative strategy is to teach clients and those early to recovery the multisensory stabilization skills in this book. If we can teach recovering individuals to listen to their bodies and emotional cues while they are in a group meeting and equip them with skills to address these disturbances, then tolerating groups or meetings with potentially disturbing subject matter becomes more realistic. See the case of Susan at the end of this chapter for a detailed explanation of how this process can play out.

I hope that after reading this chapter you have gained some enhanced insight into the nature of trauma. The parallel between physical and emotional wounds appear throughout this book because there are so many salient connections. It is important to remember that wounds heal from the inside out. As abuse survivor and singer Tori Amos once expressed, "You must crawl into your wounds to discover where your fears are, because once the bleeding starts, the cleansing can begin." It is little wonder that this quote is popular on recovery-oriented websites all over the Internet.

Many of us who entered the field of addiction treatment and the psychotherapeutic professions are familiar with the term "the wounded healer." This term, attributed to Dutch priest and writer Henri Nouwen, accurately describes many of our journeys. Nouwen (2004) once wrote, "When we honestly ask ourselves which person in our lives means the most to us, we often find that it is those who, instead of giving advice, solutions, or cures, have chosen rather to share our pain and touch our wounds with a warm and tender hand."

May we heed this wisdom as we work with the wounded.

The Case of Susan

Susan used drugs and alcohol for more than thirty years, incurring numerous life consequences as the result of her addiction: inability to finish college despite her obvious intelligence, failed relationships, financial concerns, and problems in parenting her children. Susan began using drugs and alcohol during her adolescence as a way of coping with the wounds of a traumatic childhood, having endured experiences similar to the storied *Sybil*. Although Susan's personality never split into separate alters, she relied on "zoning out" and letting her mind wander away from her body to deal with the brutal abuse that she endured at the hands of her mother.

When she entered inpatient treatment following a near-fatal overdose, Susan's motivation for change was very high; already in her forties, Susan knew that her life needed to change or she would end up dead. Although she felt treatment was working, on most days she found group work next to intolerable. She would usually "zone out" during group sharing. Sometimes the disturbances were so great that she would break down and cry, needing to leave the room. As Susan shared, it was rarely what she said in group that caused these experiences. Rather, listening to others share or going too deep into her own thoughts during the group process triggered this dissociative response. When she had about thirty days sober, Susan presented to my office, referred to me because of my specialty in treating PTSD. Susan felt a great deal of relief that I affirmed her struggle with group. Like with many treatment centers, several counselors told Susan at her rehab that she just needed to "listen up," or that what she was doing by zoning out and leaving the group was just her way of "getting attention." Through learning a series of simple, multisensory coping skills like using pressure points, the butterfly hug, and slow, bilateral tapping while she thought about a pleasant color or sensation, Susan was better able to tolerate sitting in groups and twelve-step meetings. Gaining consistency in using these skills became the foundation of Susan being able to effectively reprocess her past and move forward in sobriety.

At the Movies

One of the best ways to learn more about traumatic stress is to see it depicted in a human story. Our culture loves movies, and here is a short list of great recommendations if you want to see some representations of traumatic stress, in the Large-T and small-t forms, to expand your learning:

Enemies: A Love Story, 1989

Good Will Hunting, 1997

In the Valley of Elah, 2007

The King's Speech, 2010

The Pacific, 2010

Ray, 2004

Sarah's Key, 2010

Walk the Line, 2005

Welcome to Sarajevo, 1997

A Common List* of Problematic Trauma-Related Beliefs

Responsibility	Value
I should have known better.	I am not good enough.
I should have done something.	I am a bad person.
I did something wrong.	I am permanently damaged.
I am to blame.	I am defective.
I cannot be trusted.	I am terrible.
Safety	I am worthless/inadequate.
I cannot trust myself.	I am insignificant.
I cannot trust anyone.	I am not important.
I am in danger.	I deserve to die.
I am not safe.	I deserve only bad things.
I cannot show my emotions.	I am stupid.
Choice	I do not belong.
I am not in control.	I am different.
I have to be perfect/please everyone.	I am a failure.
I am weak.	I am ugly.
I am trapped.	My body is ugly.
I have no options.	I am alone.

Power

I cannot get what I want.

I cannot succeed.

I cannot stand up for myself.

I cannot let it out.

I am powerless/helpless.

* This list is a based on a synthesis of literature in traumatic stress studies, combined with my own clinical experiences of working with traumatized individuals. For more information about the identified domains of responsibility, safety, choice, power, and value, see Stewart-Grey (2008).

Toolkit Strategy: Exercise for Those Working with Addicted Individuals

Take about five minutes to scan "A Common List of Problematic Trauma-Related Beliefs." Then, think about the last two or three clients you have worked with who have specifically disclosed issues related to addiction or compulsive behavior. Which of these beliefs, in your assessment, might those clients "check off" as being relevant to them?

Taking the exercise a step further, consider the relevant beliefs. Do you believe that they emerged from the person's addictive behavior, or did they predate the addictive behavior? Take a few minutes to jot down your responses.

CHAPTER 4

What Twelve-Step Recovery Can Offer Traumatized Individuals

One day, Jeff (a personal friend of mine) and his friend were on their college campus, searching for a secluded spot so that they could smoke a little weed. As they walked, they saw a girl who had an obvious physical disability on a nearby pathway, heading to class in a wheelchair. The friend, obviously uncomfortable, commented on how terrible it must be for that girl to maneuver around campus in a wheelchair. Jeff responded, "Well, it looks like she's been in a wheelchair most of her life. What would be even worse is if, all of sudden, you or I found ourselves strapped to a wheelchair...we wouldn't know what to do."

Little did Jeff know that within a couple of months, his words would prove chillingly prophetic. Following a near fatal accident that was the direct result of his addiction, Jeff suffered permanent paralysis from the waist down. He was not even old enough to legally drink in his state. While he adjusted to the new realities of living his life in a wheelchair, Jeff felt embarrassed and ashamed to walk into a twelve-step recovery meeting, even though he knew deep down that he probably had to return to twelve-step meetings if he was going to stay sober. Jeff had been to twelve-step meetings during prior attempts at recovery, and he found the prospect of having to explain why he was in a wheelchair (not to mention the taunts of old-timers saying things like, "It didn't get any easier out there did it?") too overwhelming. So, for nearly a year, Jeff managed to stay sober through close supervision by his mother and adjusting to his new physical existence...but he knew that something was missing.

Jeff eventually found his way back to a twelve-step meeting, and he was welcomed back without the taunts that he feared. In the midst of taking risks and beginning to really work a program, he found that a very interesting phenomenon occurred...through sharing his story, the process of healing from his trauma was able to take place. Jeff found that as he shared one-on-one with people he formed connections with in the fellowship, took an inventory in the fourth step, and eventually shared his story in public at speaker meetings, the process of gradual catharsis took place. Jeff believes that telling his story helped with the desensitization process that so often needs to occur in trauma recovery, noting, "Every time I told the story, I felt a weight lifting." Today, eighteen years into his recovery journey, Jeff is able to share his message at twelve-step meetings and genuinely laugh when telling some of the same stories that used to bring him to tears. For Jeff, there is no doubt that his recovery from his addiction and the healing of his traumas (physical and mental) was an integrated process.

For someone like Jeff, a trauma survivor who came to embrace twelve-step programming and principles, the twelve-step approach offered more than just a recovery plan for alcoholism or addiction...it helped him heal in a holistic manner. One may argue that Jeff's case is the ideal and not the norm, and that he must have had an unusually wonderful twelve-step support system or that outside help was needed (which in Jeff's case, like in many survivors' cases, it was). However, Jeff and many other trauma survivors working twelve-step programs are quick to credit the unquestionably important structure that the twelve steps gave them in guiding their healing. Structure is one of the main benefits that recovery programs in general, not just twelve-step programs, provide for the healing process. In this chapter, we discuss what a twelve-step program can offer someone who is seeking addiction recovery but also has issues connected to unresolved trauma; we consider how many of the well-established twelve-step alternatives fit the bill for addicted survivors of trauma who are in need of a structured program. Although this chapter presents a brief overview of the history and background of the twelve steps, I do not provide an intensive primer on twelve-step philosophy largely because other sources completely cover this (see the box called Further Reading in this chapter if you are looking for such material). However, this chapter considers and discusses the specific features of twelve-step philosophy and approaches to twelve-step programming that may be specifically helpful to a traumatized person recovering from an addictive disorder.

The twelve-step approach gets a bad rap in many trauma treatment circles for being outdated and insufficient in addressing the complex needs of trauma survivors. However, in this chapter, we discuss the elements of twelve-step philosophy and approaches to recovery that, if explained to trauma survivors in a user-friendly, "meet them where they're at" manner, may actually help with recovery from the addiction and the unresolved trauma concerns simultaneously. We discuss the benefits of positive sober support that recovery fellowships can provide, the opportunities for mutual support through listening, and the flexible structure offered by the twelve steps that can serve as a blueprint of dual recovery. We also consider the facets of twelve-step approaches that allow for catharsis (specifically fourth and fifth step work and having the opportunities to share the story), and the prized philosophies of twelve-step programming (such as how to pursue a spiritual awakening, practice acceptance, and deal with resentments) that may also prove helpful in trauma recovery.

I would like to address two potential criticisms of this chapter. Certain twelve-step purists may accuse me of stretching the boundaries of the program beyond where they the originators intended it to stretch. A recovering professional challenged me once at a workshop, saying, "The twelve steps of (insert specific fellowship) are meant as a program of recovery from (insert specific substance or behavior), not trauma." Although, in a purest sense, these critics may be right; if we use the broad definition of trauma offered in chapter 3, then just about everybody walking into a recovery meeting for the first time has some level of unresolved trauma that could render them, him or her paralyzed from fully embracing a recovery program. Thus, part of addiction recovery *is* trauma recovery. Moreover, I often hear at twelve-step meetings that alcoholism, addiction, or the problematic behavior is merely the manifestation (or symptom) of a larger personality problem. My argument is that traumas can, and often do, play a critical role in shaping this larger personality problem, so approaching the twelve steps in a trauma-informed manner is beyond relevant.

The other criticism I anticipate is from professionals (or from people who have had bad experiences with twelve-step fellowships in the past) who will tell me that what I present in this chapter is the ideal, not how twelve-step programs are actually run in the real world. It is true that what I present in this chapter is the ideal, the full spectrum of what a twelve-step fellowship can offer an addicted trauma survivor. (The optimal conditions are that a survivor remains open-minded to these suggested approaches to recovery and that meetings provide a welcoming, tolerant atmosphere). Offering the addicted survivor of trauma proper, nonjudgmental support and guidance is critical. I am the first to admit that all twelve-step fellowships, meetings, and people are *not* created equally…so many newcomers to twelve-step meetings are unfortunately not greeted with the ideal I present in this chapter. Rest assured, I address these criticisms in chapter 5. For now, let's stay focused on the possibilities.

A Brief Overview of How Twelve-Step Recovery Came to Be

When I first entered recovery, two ideas from the history of Alcoholics Anonymous really made an impression upon me. The first was the idea of one alcoholic helping another alcoholic; through this mechanism of action upon which the program was founded in 1935, sharing with people who "get" us, we can receive the support that we need to heal. I felt so uniquely crazy and warped coming into recovery, it was a relief to hear people say, "It's okay, Jamie…I get where you're coming from." From an addiction and trauma perspective, that validation was incredibly healing. The second idea that appealed to me was this notion of a user-friendly spirituality as represented by the phrase *God as we understand Him*. Although some philosophical disputes took place amongst the early members of Alcoholics Anonymous before they agreed upon this phrase, the phrase eventually made its way into the twelve steps. As someone who entered recovery craving some spiritual connection but finding myself wounded by the dogmas of denomination due to my religious upbringing, I found this phrase to be embracing and welcoming, and I believe that this was the intention of the fellowship's founders.

In a nutshell, the founding of Alcoholics Anonymous traces back to 1935 when Bill Wilson, a former stockbroker from New York trying to recover his career, took a business trip to Akron, Ohio. Wilson had been sober for five months, largely using the ideas of the Oxford Groups, a nondenominational Christian organization that embraced a charism of outreach to the downtrodden. Wilson, having had a sudden spiritual awakening while recovering from alcohol withdrawal in a New York City hospital, had learned that the best way to keep what he had gained was to share it with others through outreach. In the five months following his spiritual awakening, Wilson attempted to help scores of alcoholics, mostly by preaching to them, and found that not a single one stayed sober…except for himself.

While in Akron awaiting the outcome of a proxy dispute, Wilson found himself in the lobby of the Mayflower Hotel, and the lure of the bar seemed very appealing. He knew that to stay sober, he had to talk to another alcoholic. Thus, using the pay telephone in the Mayflower lobby and the church directory posted nearby, he frantically began calling ministers to see if they could assist in his quest. Eventually, he found a minister who put him in touch with a parishioner who knew just the right person for Bill Wilson to talk to: Dr. Bob Smith. Smith, who had lost his surgical practice as the result of his alcoholism, was still actively drinking during his first meeting with Bill Wilson in May of 1935. Having also tried the Oxford Groups, Smith was initially resistant to talk to Wilson although, after several hours of simple sharing, Smith and Wilson knew that they had found something special, so they began their quest of reaching out to other alcoholics as a way to stay sober themselves.

A useful distinction I once learned is that the aim of the Oxford Groups was to reach out to everyone. However, the aim of this fellowship that would become Alcoholics Anonymous was to reach out to just the drunk. In the early years of starting up meetings in both Akron and New York, the structure of what Wilson and Smith had discovered was lacking, but slowly developing. In addition to incorporating several spiritual role models into their approach, such as English philosopher William James and St. Francis of Assisi, Wilson and Smith continued to utilize a six-step plan from the Oxford Groups:

Admitted hopelessness
Got honest with self
Got honest with another
Made amends
Help others
Prayed to God as you understand him

Wilson, with the help of others in the emerging fellowship, eventually expanded these ideas into what would eventually become the twelve steps. In 1939, Wilson put together a book that spelled out the twelve-step program, complemented by stories of those who had recovered using the approach that was developing within the fellowship meetings.

The publication of the book *Alcoholics Anonymous* officially gave the fellowship a name, saw the publication of the first draft of the twelve steps, and provided the growing AA fellowship with some uniformity. Although AA cofounder Bill Wilson is the primary author of the first part of *Alcoholics Anonymous*, various edits of the book were passed back and forth between the New York and Akron groups prior to publication. Bill Wilson (from New York) and the Akron groups wanted to keep the focus on spirituality. The New York groups wanted to keep the focus on the physical aspects of alcoholism. What emerged was a combination of the two approaches. *Alcoholics Anonymous* also featured a presentation of the disease concept of addiction by Dr. William Silkworth, the physician who treated Bill Wilson while he was in the hospital.

The groups hoped that the initial publication of the book in April of 1939 would propel the message of *Alcoholics Anonymous* into the mainstream. To the dismay of the groups, orders for the book only trickled in, following a nationwide postcard advertising blast. The Rockefeller Foundation, which provided limited support to the fellowship in its early stages, assisted with getting the four thousand non-purchased copies of the book out of storage. It was actually Jack

Alexander's *Saturday Evening Post* article in March of 1941 that resulted in an exponential expansion in *Alcoholics Anonymous* membership throughout the United States. Famed writer Alexander set out to expose AA as a fraud; however, what emerged were six pages of praise about what he observed in the AA fellowship, necessitating a second printing of *Alcoholics Anonymous* in 1941. Some fruits of AA's establishment included more widespread acceptance of alcoholism as a disease (including acceptance by the American Medical Association by the early 1950s). Additionally, AA and the twelve steps inspired what would come to be known as the Minnesota model of treatment, which brought twelve-step approaches (although not the specific fellowship of AA) into hospital-based treatment centers around the country. By the 1950s, not only had treatment programs started to grow, but also a variety of other fellowships, such as Narcotics Anonymous and Al-Anon Family Groups, began to form using the twelve-step approach. To date, hundreds of recovery fellowships use the original twelve steps of Alcoholics Anonymous, including several that specifically target trauma, incest, and assault recovery. If you are interested in reading more about the history, development, and fruits of Alcoholics Anonymous and/or twelve-step recovery, consider checking out some of the sources listed in "For Further Reading."

For Further Reading: Books

Adams, A.J. (2009). *Undrunk: A skeptic's guide to Alcoholics Anonymous.* Center City, MN: Hazelden.

Alcoholics Anonymous World Services. (1957). *Alcoholics anonymous comes of age.* New York: Author.

Alcoholics Anonymous World Services. (1973). *As Bill sees it: The A.A. way of life (selected writings from A.A.'s co-founder).* New York: Author.

Alcoholics Anonymous World Services. (1980). *Dr. Bob and the good oldtimers.* New York: Author.

Alcoholics Anonymous World Services. (2001). *Alcoholics Anonymous.* (4th ed.). New York: Author.

Anonymous. (1993). *The dual disorders recovery book.* Center City, MN: Hazelden.

The Augustine Fellowship. (1986). *Sex and love addicts anonymous.* Author.

Cocaine Anonymous World Services, Inc. (2004). *Hope, faith, and courage.* Los Angeles, CA: Author.

Gamblers Anonymous International Service Office. *G.A. big book: Sharing recovery through gambler's anonymous.* Los Angeles, CA: Author.

Kurtz, E. (1991). *Not God: A history of Alcoholics Anonymous.* Center City, MN: Hazelden.

Marshall, S. (2003). *Young, sober, and free.* (2nd ed.) Center City, MN: Hazelden.

Narcotics Anonymous World Services. (1991). *Narcotics Anonymous.* (5th ed.). Van Nuys, CA: Author.

Nowinski, J., & Baker, S. (2003). *The twelve-step facilitation handbook.* (2nd ed.) Center City, MN: Hazelden.

Overeaters Anonymous, Inc. (2001). *Overeaters anonymous.* (2nd ed.) Rio Rancho, New Mexico: Author.

Samples, P., & Hamilton, T. (1994). *The twelve steps and dual disorders.* Center City, MN: Hazelden.

White, W. (1998). *Slaying the dragon: The history of addiction treatment and recovery in America.* Bloomington, IL: Chestnut Ridge Health Systems.

World Service Office for Al-Anon and Alateen. (1995). *How Al-Anon works for families and friends of alcoholics.* Virginia Beach, VA: Author.

For Further Reading: Websites

Hazelden (Bookstore): www.hazelden.org

Mitchell, K. (2006). Writing the big book: History of the writing of Alcoholics Anonymous: http://alcoholism.about.com/cs/history/a/blmitch8.htm

Recovery Emporium: www.recoveryemporium.com

Recovery Universe: www.recoveryuniverse.com

Serenity Found: www.serenityfound.org

TIP: Use Google or the Internet search engine of your choice to access the official websites of the fellowships you might like to read more about. Most official sites, present the history of each respective fellowship.

What Twelve-Step Fellowships Offer in Terms of Sober, Mutual Support

In treating trauma-related disorders, regardless of whether or not the person struggles with an addictive disorder, it is important that stabilization take place. As discussed in chapter 2, a wise treatment provider would not expect a person who is new to recovery (whether that be from the addiction, the trauma, or both) to address the root disturbances associated with their traumatic stress unless a person has a set of coping skills to help him self-soothe in a healthy way. Developing a healthy, mutual support, for so many addicted survivors of trauma is a critical component of stabilization. Positive trauma-related social support is important in the development of a strong, early therapeutic alliance; lack of support is one of the strongest predictors in the development of PTSD (Keller, Zollner, & Feeny, 2010).

The benefits of mutual support offered by twelve-step groups are twofold: first, many individuals entering recovery are surrounded by friends and family who are not sober or otherwise healthy, so the meetings can offer an outlet to start building a network of people who support the individual's recovery. Second, because isolation due to shame is such a common phenomenon with both recovering addicts/alcoholics and traumatized individuals, many people enter recovery believing that the behaviors they engaged in or the feelings they experience are some unique brand of crazy or defective. Hearing others share similar experiences, thoughts, and feelings at meetings facilitates the healing process. In hearing others share, many addicted survivors hear messages that help convey more positive beliefs in the vein of "You are not alone."

For many, once they address some of the barriers about opening up to others (solutions for these barriers will be discussed in chapters 6 and 7), getting involved with people in a twelve-step fellowship becomes a powerful mechanism of action in the healing process. After Mae, an African-American woman in her late forties who was the survivor of childhood sexual abuse, got over the initial social barrier of getting involved with the groups, the benefits were astounding:

I am not a social butterfly, so that means that I have to put myself in the fellowship—my fellowship is Alcoholics Anonymous—I had to put myself in the middle and start interacting with people, and I kept missing that. I kept missing that it always got worse and never better.

At the time of a treatment follow-up interview, Mae credited the involvement in her fellowship and the receipt of outside counseling help as vital in her attaining six and a half years of sobriety, the most she had ever experienced in her long history of attempts (Marich, 2010). For JoElle, also an African-American woman and survivor of domestic violence, involvement with twelve-step recovery groups allows her to measure her progress and remember where she has come from in her journey whenever she gets to interact with a newcomer.

People have differing reasons for wanting to make friends and support contacts within twelve-step fellowships. For Michelle, a young college student who grew up in a home with significant emotional abuse and family discord, most of her peer group consisted of people who drank, especially because she lived on campus. By coming to meetings, she was able to connect with other people who did not drink, and thus found a totally new social outlet for herself. Once she met her need for sober social interaction, she was gradually able to benefit from listening and sharing with the people in her new network of friends. What is interesting is that I have even heard critics of AA admit that as long as a person can find a reasonable meeting, at the very least, AA offers a social outlet that is preferable to going to a bar. However, for people with social needs in early recovery, the opportunities for socialization that AA offers cannot be underestimated.

Flexible Structure

At first glance, the term flexible structure might seem like an oxymoron. Upon further exploration in this chapter, we will see how flexible structure is exactly what the twelve steps offer (provided that a person who is not rigid interprets them). Moreover, flexible structure is what an addicted survivor of trauma may need to obtain solid footing on the road to recovery.

In my investigation of addiction recovery programs, which includes programs informed by the twelve steps, programs that have nothing to do with the twelve steps, and programs that blend approaches, one common denominator seems to emerge in what makes a successful addiction-recovery program: lifestyle change. Many individuals who have recovered from addictions contend that having structure was an absolutely critical element in making this change happen (Fletcher, 2001; White & Kurz, 2006). Consider the case of Vince. A white male in his early thirties, Vince found himself in a place where he had lost everything as a result of his alcoholism: his girlfriend, his house, his business, and his driver's license. Without insurance, and having burned too many bridges at the community-based treatment facility in his area, Vince's only choice for structured treatment was to go to a Christian-based facility in a nearby town. Interestingly, Vince was an agnostic, but he somehow knew that he needed to go away somewhere for ninety days and "get back on track." Vince credits the structure that the Christian facility gave him in initiating his sobriety. "I didn't buy a word of what they were saying spiritually, but the structure I received there made all the difference."

While the importance of structure in bringing about lifestyle change is important, we must also consider that people growing up in traumatic environments may respond to structure in different ways. Some people like the regimen because it is familiar to them; however, others feel completely turned off by structures, order, and being told what to do. That's the tricky thing about trauma: its effects on a person are varied and unpredictable. Hence, the flexibility concept, or the ability to meet a person where he or she is "at" during any given point in his or her recovery becomes vital.

If not approached with a rigid mindset, so many facets of the twelve steps, not to mention the principles espoused by other recovery programs, are incredibly flexible. For instance, the traditions of Alcoholics Anonymous state that "the only requirement for membership is a desire to stop drinking" (Alcoholics Anonymous, 2001). Thus, a person who is afraid to come to a meeting because he fears he will have to introduce himself as an alcoholic or work the twelve steps can be assured that none of that is required to take part in AA...it is simply suggested. Most twelve-step programs are suggestive only. Now, I'm the first to admit that some very rigid-minded sponsors have lost this idea along the way somehow and have turned the suggestions into absolute orders. However, for a person who is resistant to structure and order, especially if this resistance is trauma-related, being assured that the components of the program and the steps are *suggestive only* can make all the difference. From a trauma-sensitive perspective, it can actually help with one's sense of personal empowerment by making a personal choice to take the suggestions.

Many addicted survivors of trauma choose to take the suggestion of working the twelve steps. Although traumatized people tend to have problems with some wording in the twelve steps (discussed in chapter 5), there are other language choices in the steps that allow for great flexibility and tolerance in meeting the newcomer. Let's look at some specific examples:

Step 1: We admitted that we were powerless over alcohol, that our lives had become unmanageable. While many survivors and otherwise resistant people struggle with the term *powerless*, the step does not say that we are powerless people. It simply says that we are powerless when it comes to alcohol, drugs, etc. The distinction is an important one in helping to meet people where they are *at* when coming into recovery.

Step 3: Made a decision to turn our will and our lives over to the care of God *as we understand Him*. That italicized phrase makes all the difference...it gives people who work a twelve step program permission to fire their old concept of God and what he/she/it means to them if it has not helped them to stay sober. Some people of an agnostic temperament who cannot embrace spirituality choose to use God as "Good Orderly Direction" or "Group of Drunks." Although some twelve-step groups and sponsors may misinterpret the step, in its truest form, it leaves it up to the individual to decide how he or she will see this Higher Power, an idea that is incredibly flexible.

Step 5: Admitted to God, to ourselves, and to another human being the exact nature of our wrongs. So many people get hung up on this step, which we discuss in greater depth in the next chapter. However, let's examine the flexibility inherent in this step. It doesn't say that you need to voice your wrongs to a sponsor, a priest, a minister, a counselor, or to the whole world—it simply says "another human being." The person working the step chooses who that human being is, and it is a decision she can make based on her own comfort and safety levels.

Step 9: Made direct amends to such people whenever possible except when to do so would injure them or others. The beauty in this step is that it is not an absolute step. Making things right, or making amends, is part of the suggested twelve-step process. However, this step acknowledges that there are certain cases in which seeking people out to make amends might make things worse. Most people interpret this step to mean that the person working the step is also included in the phrase "injure them or others."

Step 11: Sought through prayer and meditation to improve our conscious contact with God *as we understand Him*, praying only for a knowledge of His will for our lives and the power to carry it out. Once again, the flexible property in this step is in the italics… it is up to the person working the step to decide.

Opportunities for Catharsis

Catharsis, often defined as the purging of emotions, comes from the Latin root meaning, "to cleanse." This process is usually required on some level for meaningful recovery to occur… this applies to addiction recovery, trauma recovery, or combined recovery. The task of processing trauma that we discussed in chapter 3 implies some form of catharsis, be it verbal, physical, emotional, spiritual, or a combination of approaches. Many individuals dread the catharsis of recovery because they fear it will make them worse, or because it's a process, like taking out the trash or doing other chores, that people simply dread.

Allow me to share a metaphor that I often present to my clients. Unresolved emotions, thoughts, and experiences are like items in a kitchen garbage can that you never empty out. You may continue to stuff them down into the garbage can, but eventually it will overflow and start to stink up the kitchen. Temporary fixes like air freshener and pushing the garbage down farther into the can may help the state of the kitchen in the short term, but nothing is going to help like getting that garbage out to the curb. In real life, the garbage man does not come into your house to take your garbage out for you…it is up to you to take the garbage out to the curb. Only then can "the garbage man," be it your Higher Power, your support group, the universe, or however you choose to see it, take the stuff away, freeing you of its power.

There are many opportunities within twelve-step and other recovery programs to engage in catharsis. In a twelve-step model, steps four and five provide a golden opportunity for such catharsis. We discuss in chapter 5 how these steps prove to be a gauntlet for so many people in recovery. However, with proper preparation and guidance in working the first three steps (together with some outside help if needed), steps four and five do not have to be frightening; in fact, they can be quite healing. Steps four and five ask the recovering individual to take a searching and fearless moral inventory and share that inventory with God/Higher Power, him or herself, and just one other human being. If done sensitively, steps four and five can be a powerful form of narrative therapy that allows the addicted survivor of trauma to get all of the garbage out.

As Jeff, the recovering trauma survivor whose case opened this chapter, shared:

> Steps four and five allow you to identify the causes and conditions of your disease and all that has happened as a result of it. These steps allow you to identify old ideas, so many of which happened as a result of trauma. What's interesting is that so many people don't even realize that they have been traumatized by their addiction until they do steps four and five.

Jeff's insights are powerful in explaining the potential for healing that working these steps can offer, if the recovering person chooses to work them.

Although steps four and five are the clearest examples of how the power of catharsis can help, in a broader sense, all of the steps can play some type of role in catharsis if they allow the recovering person to get something out and work it through. Every night before I go to sleep, I offer my prayers using the tenth and eleventh steps as guides. I go through my day with God, admit where I could have done better, and turn stressors over, asking him to reveal his will to me. At least for me, this ritual is a form of daily catharsis that I cannot live without.

As Jeff's case highlighted, outside of working the steps, there are ample opportunities in twelve-step fellowships or other types of recovery groups for a person to experience catharsis by telling his or her story. Whether you're in a restaurant having coffee with your sponsor and some friends after the meeting, talking to a member of your support group on the phone in a moment of emotional revelation, or getting up to the podium and sharing your story publicly at a meeting, healing can happen through telling your story. At least this idea is what Bill Wilson and Bob Smith tapped into when they founded Alcoholics Anonymous. It's no wonder that there is a great deal of buzz in trauma treatment circles about an approach to treatment called *narrative therapy*, or healing through telling the story (White & Epston, 1990). Narrative therapy is an approach that AA, other twelve-step groups, and many other recovery programs have been incorporating all along to facilitate healing.

Other Gems

As a therapist specializing primarily in the treatment of trauma, I have the privilege of hearing about the latest therapies available to help our clients work on their goals. Two therapies that have garnered a great deal of attention in recent years are dialectical behavioral therapy (DBT), an approach that combines cognitive behavioral therapy approaches together with principles of Buddhist meditation, and acceptance and commitment therapy (ACT), a similar approach using principles of mindfulness. What makes me chuckle, as someone who has worked a twelve-step program for quite some time, is that both of these therapies contain "repackaged" applications of many sobriety strategies that AA and other twelve-step programs have long incorporated. One of the central skills in both of these therapies is the importance of radical acceptance, a concept that receives a great deal of attention in the book *Alcoholics Anonymous* and that other fellowships emphasize.

Practicing acceptance is a strategy that the steps do not directly reference (although the steps can certainly help with this process); however, it is a suggestion that twelve-step recovery settings often make. A classic passage in the book *Alcoholics Anonymous* simply yet completely defines acceptance and how to "work it" as a recovery tool:

> And acceptance is the answer to all my problems today. When I am disturbed, it is because I find some person, place, thing or situation—some fact of my life—unacceptable to me, and I can find no serenity until I accept that person, place, thing or situation as being exactly the way it is supposed to be at this moment. Nothing, absolutely nothing happens in God's world by mistake. Until I could accept my alcoholism, I could not stay sober; unless I accept life completely on life's terms, I cannot be happy. I need to concentrate not so much on what needs to be changed in the world as on what needs to be changed in me and in my attitudes (Alcoholics Anonymous World Services, 2001; p. 417).

As a recovering person and as a counselor, I find that this passage, if read, studied, and applied, offers an ideal solution for helping a trauma survivor move out of victim mode and into survivor mode.

Accepting something, someone, or some situation does *not* mean that you have to like it. For instance, you can accept the fact that your father abused you, or that you witnessed unspeakable horrors during a terrorist event, without endorsing the actions. You don't even have to embrace the spiritually saccharine idea that *everything happens for a reason*. All the principle of acceptance asks you to do is to internalize that it happened, and there's nothing you can do to change the fact that it happened. So often, people struggle with their pasts, especially the difficult relationships that the past may contain, and beat themselves up with internal phrases like, "If only things could have been different," or, "If only she would (or could) just change." In essence, the trauma survivor is putting all the power on the other person. Practicing acceptance actually allows for personal empowerment. Although you're not letting the person off the hook for what might have occurred, you are making a conscious choice to take your life back and focus on what you can control when you practice acceptance.

Consider the case of Frances. A young woman in her early twenties, Frances grew up in a broken home with an alcoholic mother, in addition to surviving severe childhood bullying in her Catholic elementary school. For years prior to entering recovery for her own alcoholism, Frances was admittedly "other-focused." Frances shares:

> I would spend so much mental energy, trying to will my mother into changing, or trying to will my boyfriend into loving me more. I would say things like, "Things will get better when she changes," or "My life will be fine once he makes those changes," and I stayed miserable, drinking to cope with it all, just waiting around for them. In my early months in the program, I was introduced to the concept of acceptance, specifically the line that acceptance is the answer to all my problems today. For me, it felt like the most radical piece of advice I ever received. Suddenly it dawned on me, "They just are who they are. Accept it. Now it's up to you to change you and live your life without waiting for them."

Frances's story is a prime example of how acceptance can be a helpful concept with both addiction recovery and trauma recovery, especially if one sees it as a measure of empowerment.

Another classic suggestion presented in the book *Alcoholics Anonymous* and used in other fellowships is how to deal with resentments. Resentment comes from the Latin roots *re* and *sentire*, which literally mean "to feel again." (Hmm…kind of sounds like what happens with trauma, no?) Resentments are the grudges that we hold against other people or situations. Not being able to let go of them can be harder than it seems if the root cause of the resentment was a traumatic experience, the aftereffects of which stayed locked in that limbic brain we discussed in chapter 3. If a recovering person is willing to accept a spiritual approach to dealing with a resentment, a very powerful suggestion appears in the book *Alcoholics Anonymous*:

If you have resentment you want to be free of, if you will pray for the person or thing that you resent, you will be free. If you will ask in prayer for everything you want for yourself to be given to them, you will be free. Ask for their health, their prosperity, their happiness, and you will be free. Even when you don't really want it for them and your prayers are only words and you don't mean it, go ahead and do it anyway. Do it everyday for two weeks, and you will find you have come to mean it and to want it for them, and you will realize that where you used to feel bitterness and resentment and hatred, you now feel compassionate understanding and love (Alcoholics Anonymous World Services, 2001; p. 552).

Once again, this is a suggestion and not an absolute; a trauma survivor does not have to follow these suggestions if he or she does not feel ready. However, I find that this spiritual solution has great power if a person is willing to try it. What is remarkably flexible about this suggestion is that it tells you that even if you don't mean the prayer for the person, you still do it; you *fake it 'til you make it*, so to speak.

Frances, who shared about the power of acceptance, also remarked how working this resentment prayer with the people in her life she held the biggest grudges over, specifically her father, worked for her:

> When I started praying it, it seemed a little bit weird to me. I was raised thinking you couldn't pray for a person unless you meant it. I stepped out of my comfort zone and gave this a try. When I first started praying it for my father, I didn't mean a word of it, and I even got a little feisty with God. "Dear God," I would pray, "Please help that evil man and give him every prosperity that I want for myself." I would even throw in a few choice swear words here and there! It took a lot longer than two weeks on the big ones, like my dad or one of my other abusers, but eventually, I found that this prayer helped me release the power these people held in my head.

Clearly, praying the resentment prayer is not for everyone when first entering a recovery program, and it may be a tough sell on some trauma survivors. However, with time and some willingness, if a person chooses to try it, it can be very empowering because the person praying it actively releases the power this other person has over her. Thus, she can become free to live a life without the abuser still wielding conscious control. I see this resentment prayer strategy as the power of the pardon in action.

Whatever Works

Although I personally endorse twelve-step principles, I am realistic enough to admit that twelve-step programming will not work for everyone. There are dozens of recovery programs and paths available in the modern era that offer alternatives to the twelve-step approach, and many of them are outstanding. As a professional, I am looking for two major elements should one of my patients seek out an alternative fellowship: One, does the program promote healthy lifestyle change within the individual person, helping him to reach and maintain his recovery goals? And two, is the program helping the person reach his recovery goals in a way that is not shaming, taking into account the sum total of his life experiences, including any traumatic elements?

The Internet is a treasure trove of resources for pointing you and the people you work with toward twelve-step alternatives for recovery within your community. Simply entering "twelve-step alternatives" into a search engine will offer many possibilities. If you are so inclined to seek these out for your own benefit or for the benefit of those you work with, I encourage you to use these two questions as a guide. Many of the recovery programs out there promote themselves in a way that puts down twelve steps or reliance on a Higher Power, and I generally get concerned whenever I see this level of negativity. It's kind of like the religion or the political ideology that promotes what they have to offer simply by putting down the other side. Look for programs that are positive in their language. Also, be aware of the programs that not only put down twelve steps or traditional recovery but also promise to offer quick solutions that seem too good to be true. One of the principles of trauma-informed recovery, supported by our primer on trauma in chapter 3, is that proper healing takes time. Please consult the next For Further Reading list if you would like to expand your knowledge base in this area.

For Further Reading

Fletcher, A. (2001). *Sober for good: New solutions for drinking problems—advice from those who have succeeded.* New York: Houghton Mifflin.

Solomon, M. (2008). *AA not the only way: Your one stop resource guide to twelve-step alternatives.* (2nd ed.) Venice, CA: Capalo Press.

Volpicelli, J. & Szalavitz, M. (2000). *Recovery options: The complete guide.* New York: Wiley & Sons.

In this section, and throughout this chapter, I present a small sampling of how the twelve steps and strategies associated with twelve-step programming can not only help trauma survivors recover from their addiction concerns, but may also help in resolving the residual effects of the trauma. I also present a trauma-informed litmus test to evaluate alternatives to twelve-step programming that may prove helpful in facilitating meaningful, recovery-oriented lifestyle change. Proper guidance impacts the success of these strategies with traumatized people, be it from a sponsor or a professional. We explore in-depth reflections on the role of trauma-sensitive counseling and sponsorship in further chapters. As demonstrated in this chapter, there is more flexibility in what the twelve-step approach is intended to be than many give twelve-step programs credit for.

Toolkit Strategy: Evaluating Twelve-Step Alternatives

Enter "twelve-step alternatives" or "AA alternatives" into an Internet search engine of your choice and scan your search results, choosing a program that jumps out at you (e.g., SMART Recovery, Rational Recovery, LifeRing, Celebrate Recovery, Moderation Management, etc.). Take a few moments to explore the program you chose, reading the program's philosophy and approach. Then, apply the "litmus test" questions presented in this chapter to what you found:

1. *Does this program seem have the potential to promote healthy lifestyle change and help a person reach and maintain his recovery goals?*

2. *Does this program have the potential to help a person reach her recovery goals in a way that is not shaming, taking into account the sum total of her life experiences, including any traumatic elements?*

CHAPTER 5

Where Twelve-Step Recovery Can (and Often Does) Go Wrong

I magine that you grew up in a home where "don't talk, don't trust, and don't feel" were the unwritten rules. You witnessed unspeakable abuse between your father and your mother, and even though you had so many emotional needs that must be addressed, your mother quite literally raged on you whenever you went to her for help. She yelled at you if you cried; she belittled you if you spoke up. So even though you were experiencing horrific abuse at the hands of an uncle, who was a respected leader in the fundamentalist church your family attended, you knew that you dared not speak. Yet the feelings were unbearable, and they had no way to get out. In fact, you believed that letting out your feelings might put your life in danger. So in your early teens, when several of your peers at school invited you to try a little alcohol and weed with them, you quickly learned that these substances not only helped you to deal with the feelings, but they also allowed you to better cope with the pressure of having to hold in so many feelings. Eventually, because your body was vulnerable to developing the disease of addiction (your family history with the disease was extensive), the little bit of alcohol and weed turned into daily use of cocaine, and soon heroin entered the mix.

Now twenty-two, you enter your first recovery program for addiction after getting into some legal problems. As part of your program, you are required to attend Alcoholics Anonymous meetings. At your first meeting, which a lot of "old timers" and traditionalists populate, you hear this phrase: "Take the cotton out of your ears and put it into your mouth." Unaware of the intention behind that statement, you start to panic, start to feel that same uncomfortable, *here we go again* experience—I'm not allowed to speak up. So instead of paying attention to the meeting, you zone out, flooded by so many memories of the past. Countless times, you wanted to open your mouth and speak up about the horrors you experienced and witnessed, but you knew that you would receive punishment for it. Now here you are, at a program designed to help you, and they are telling you to do the same thing.

Reading this passage, many of you probably think I've got it all wrong. You may be saying, "She misconstrued what that slogan is supposed to mean. That slogan means that it's time that you start listening to others and taking their suggestions about what it takes to be clean." True, traditionalists may have good *intentions* when they relay such "tough love" slogans, but remember what we discussed about the nature of trauma and how it affects people—it has so little to do with the logical part of the brain. Thus, so many slogans that people in twelve-step and other recovery programs use that may seem helpful to the rational mind may do more harm than good to those with unresolved traumatic memories. As Nancy shared in chapter 2, those who have been affected by trauma "can't put anything into proper perspective." Thus, if someone introduces one of the slogans or steps to a newcomer out of context, which often happens at recovery meetings, a retraumatizing experience can occur. Pejorative, problematic slogans are just one facet of recovery programs that may prove to be problematic for those struggling with traumatic stress issues. The purpose of this chapter is to fully explore some of these problem areas. In addition to the slogans, I also address problems with step work and issues with unhealthy or dictatorial meeting styles and sponsorship as they relate to individuals affected by trauma.

Slogans

Most of the slogans heard at recovery meetings are not actually in basic texts or major pieces of literature associated with an individual fellowship. Rather, we can describe slogans as sayings, mottoes, or bite-size pieces of wisdom that have trickled down through the years in the rooms of recovery fellowships. A slogan can be helpful, especially if it resonates, or "clicks," with a person. Additionally, newcomers and old timers alike may be much more likely to remember a small saying like "Let go and let God" during a troubled moment, whereas an entire book passage or step may seem overwhelming. However, the benefit that slogans can provide because they are so compact can also prove to be a detriment. The word *slogan*, interestingly enough, comes from the same Gaelic root as the word *slew*, as in a short jab or application of brute force during a time of war. This word origin proves to be interesting because, for a newcomer struggling with trauma issues, so many slogans can be received as little jabs…jabs that can prove retraumatizing if the meaning, intention, and context are not explained.

In my work over the years with clients and research subjects, I have found the following slogans to be most problematic for recovering individuals struggling with unresolved trauma:

"Just for Today"/"One Day at a Time"
"Think, Think, Think"/"Think the Drink Through"
"Your Best Thinking Got You Here"/"Stinkin' Thinkin'"
"We Are Only as Sick as Our Secrets"
"Take the Cotton Out of Your Ears and Put it in Your Mouth"

Let's take a look at each slogan, consider its original intention, and discuss—considering what was covered about the nature of trauma in chapter 3—how each slogan may be counterproductive or otherwise problematic to a person with unresolved trauma.

Just for today/One day at a time. The concept sounds so incredibly simple…stay in today. Addicted individuals are notorious for dwelling in the past or projecting into the future, so any variation of these slogans attempts to get the addicted person to focus only on the task at hand, getting through the individual day clean and sober, and not stress about the past or future. "One day at a time" is arguably the one twelve-step slogan that people outside of twelve-step fellowships most commonly associate with recovery programs. No doubt, living in today, staying in today, operating just for today, or taking life one day at a time are excellent goals to work toward. Here is the problem: living in today can be nearly impossible for a person with unresolved trauma because what happened ten, twenty, or even fifty years ago can seem just as real as if it were happening today. Remember what author Lily Burana (2009) shared: "The long-range result is that the peace of mind you deserve in the present is held hostage by the terror of your past" (p. 227). Indeed, this passage makes sense if you consider how the limbic brain works, specifically the regulatory amygdala. I once heard it explained that the amygdala is the part of the brain that has no clock. So, when a person new to recovery who has yet to work through her issues with unresolved trauma cannot stay in today, there is a valid reason for it. Hence, a person can work on "one day at a time" as a goal, but it isn't necessarily an instant solution to a newcomer.

Think, think, think/Think the drink through. Like so many slogans, the cognitive-behavioral intention here is good…wouldn't it be nice if, when faced with the temptation to drink or use, we could all just calmly, rationally sit down and intelligently examine the consequences of our impulsive actions. However, basic understanding of how triggers work in the limbic brain with both unresolved trauma and addiction (as covered in chapter 3) suggests that these *think* slogans may be a good goal to work toward. However, as solutions in and of themselves, they are simply not adequate, especially for people who are in crisis or who are grappling with unresolved trauma. Remember, when a person is triggered, the R-complex and limbic brains take over (the sectors that regulate survival and emotion), and the neocortex, which contains our rational brain, essentially goes offline. When a person is triggered, activated, or in some state of emotional over-drive, appealing to the rational brain is a fruitless exercise *unless* some measures have been taken to first soothe or calm the limbic-level activity (more on this in chapter 6).

Your best thinking got you here/Stinkin' thinkin'. While we're on the subject of *thinking*, let's discuss these well-intentioned, but often problematic slogans. As simple logic would suggest, one of the key problems may be the contradictory nature of the think slogans. A newcomer may hear, "Hmm, on one hand they're telling me to think the drink through, but on the other hand they're telling me that I'm full of stinkin' thinkin'…well, which is it?" That whole concept of "thinking" can really be a brain twist, can't it?

Once again, the intention is good. We can often describe the thinking that fuels addictive processes, especially the defense mechanisms of rationalization, intellectualizing, and minimizing addicts often use as disordered and problematic. However, people who are new to recovery often hear these slogans as all-or-nothing proclamations; they may hear, "my thinking is all screwed up, it's all bad." The reality is that, for many survivors of trauma, they had to think on their toes after first coping with some heavy emotional experiences to stay alive and well. We often hear about the ingenuity that survivors called upon to cope against unspeakable odds in situations of natural dis-asters or war. While serving in Bosnia, I heard countless stories of how people trapped in Sarajevo during the four-year siege of the city devised to feed themselves and carry out the basic functions of survival. These testimonies on the survivor spirit continue to astonish me. Indeed, the reality of a traumatized existence can spawn some pretty creative thinking, fueled by that survival drive.

Consider, for instance, the teenage daughter whose mother was always out of the house drinking and using. Abandoned and left with a world of emotional hurt, she had to resort to any measure she knew to keep her three younger siblings fed; this often included stealing, or as she got a little bit older, dealing some marijuana to her friends. This teenage daughter knew how to cook, clean, and help the younger children with their homework, showing a great deal of resilience and smart thinking to keep everything in the house afloat. Although she went on to develop a series of problems with substance abuse and interpersonal relationships, there was a lot that she did that was *right* in her thinking to keep herself and her siblings functioning. Trauma survivors often have a great deal of pride in the thinking they mustered, albeit fueled by survival, and hearing the nature of their thinking criticized in meetings or treatment groups, especially when done in the form of an out-of-context jab like in these slogans, can be hurtful or alienating.

We are only as sick as our secrets. The intention of this slogan is that whatever we hold in—emotions, shame-based details of our past, fears—will inevitably keep us stuck and unable to move forward in recovery. If you actually consider the logic of trauma processing covered in chapter 3, this idea makes a great deal of sense. Once again, the problem largely rests with the construction of this slogan and its delivery to the newcomer. For survivors of trauma, keeping secrets is often an essential component of survival. One of the greatest tactics used by abusers is some variation of the line, "If you tell anyone at all, then I'm going to (insert threat here)." People in twelve-step meetings, or even those who work in treatment centers, often fail to consider the power of that word *secret*. Yes, an ultimate goal for healthy recovery would be for those dark, shame-filled secrets to be released in a healthy context (e.g., with a sponsor, counselor, or through a fifth step); however, it is important to consider the survival-laden context of *keeping a secret* to many newcomers struggling with unresolved trauma. Again, it is important to be gentle and not to deliver this well-intended wisdom as an insulting jab.

Take the cotton out of your ears and put it in your mouth. Of all the twelve-step slogans out there, this is the one that I like the least (which is why I opened the chapter with this slogan as an example). Although I recognize the intention of this slogan, that in early recovery it is important to listen to suggestions and not be so quick to defend ourselves and perhaps use words to rationalize our way out of recovery, its wording and delivery are downright insulting. For one young woman that participated in a major research project of mine (Marich, 2010), hearing this slogan upon entering treatment or meetings immediately caused her to shut down because, in it, she heard that what she had to say was not important. Hence, the messages of *don't talk, don't trust, and don't feel* that were given to her in her alcoholic home of origin were further enforced.

Now, I'm not discounting the importance of having newcomers gently mentored in distinguishing between what is appropriate and not appropriate to share at meetings, nor am I opposed to having newcomers appropriately confronted about when they may be using too much talk to avoid addressing some real issues and emotions. However, I am asking you to consider how *insulting* this slogan can sound to a person who is struggling to cope and work through a legacy of trauma. Taking it a step further, what if a trauma survivor was placed in a situation where he was quite literally gagged or restrained (which is common with many survivors of sexual abuse), or what if a sexual abuse survivor was ever put in a situation of having to perform forced oral sex? Just consider what hearing such a slogan out of context may mean to such an individual.

The other issue to consider with this slogan is that we encourage recovering individuals to open up about their emotional lives, and indeed, many newcomers to recovery come into treatment programs or meetings needing to unload a heavy burden. Meetings, step work, treatment programs, and various other modalities can be ideal in helping the newcomer do this, and yes, newcomers need guidance in which forums are best for opening up about which elements of their lives. However, it is important to consider how hearing this slogan at the wrong time, delivered in the wrong manner, might cause a person to shut down and perhaps never feel safe sharing in a recovery setting.

In this section, I present the most potentially problematic slogans, informed by struggles that others have shared with me. This list is by no means exhaustive; just about any recovery slogan can be problematic for a newcomer struggling with unresolved trauma if the newcomer does not understand the context of the slogan. Furthermore, the newcomer may feel like she is trying to voice a legitimate concern and she finds herself being "cut off" by and placated with a slogan. If this "cutting off" experience happens in a public way during a meeting or treatment group itself, it can be even more shaming to the individual. It is also important to consider how some individuals who are not ready, willing, or able to entertain the spiritual principles of twelve-step recovery or other faith-based recovery programs may also feel triggered if they constantly hear spiritual slogans that they are not quite ready to entertain. Some other problematic slogans that I have heard for traumatized people struggling with spirituality (especially those whose unresolved trauma may stem from an experience in a religious denomination, with a clergy member, or with an overzealous parent) include "Let go and let God," "This too shall pass," and "Nothing happens in God's world by mistake."

The Twelve Steps

In the previous chapter, we covered some of the historical foundations of the twelve steps, and discussed the benefits that following them in their suggested order can have for alcoholics and addicts. I am not arguing that the twelve steps require alteration in any way for addicted survivors of trauma. Rather, I am suggesting that the steps may be a harder sell on those with significantly unresolved trauma either because of wording that can trigger heavy emotional responses or because of what the step is asking a person to do. Here, we explore each step and the problems that each may cause for an addicted survivor of trauma. The greatest struggles seem to come with language and wording. Problems of misinterpretation are common, especially because of trauma survivors' tendency to be overly sensitive to triggering stimuli, and because those with unresolved trauma often lack the ability to put new learning into proper perspective. We will also consider how rigid application of each step may be counterproductive if we do not take a trauma survivor's unique concerns into account. I cover the solutions for what to do about these various concerns in chapter 6.

STEP I: We admitted that we were powerless over alcohol and that our lives had become unmanageable. By its very nature, a traumatic experience can render a person powerless. If the residual effects of the trauma are not resolved, a person can find herself living in a pervasive state of powerlessness, helplessness, or paralyzing fear. The language of powerlessness in step one poses one of the greatest concerns of mental health professionals who work with recovering addicts/alcoholics. As a colleague of mine expressed once, "Our job is to get a trauma survivor to tap into her personal sense of power, and here this step is telling her that she is powerless." My colleague's comments parallel those that I have heard from many trauma survivors trying to work a twelve-step program. And thus, we have one of the great semantic debates of recovery: What does it mean to be *powerless*? Are we asking the individual to admit his powerlessness just over drugs and alcohol, or over everything else in his life? And if he only admits he's powerless over drugs, alcohol, or other problematic behaviors, isn't that a belittling idea that goes against the very essence of empowerment?

Those questions are very deep and can certainly make one's head spin! Let me state here that the purpose of this book is not to entertain the philosophical implications of these questions because that would even make my head spin. The reality is, survivors of trauma coming into twelve-step recovery regularly ask themselves some variations of these questions, and without proper guidance to make sense of it all, the confusion can be alienating. Proper guidance in working the step is one of the solutions discussed in chapter 6.

The other word that trauma survivors often struggle with is *unmanageability*, especially those survivors who truly see themselves as *survivors*—people who have been able to muddle through, cope, and stay alive despite the odds placed against them. Such survivors may take offense to others calling their lives unmanageable. Additionally, those individuals who have been able to succeed in many areas of their life despite the bad things that have happened to them, even though the drinking or using may be wreaking havoc on other areas of their life, tend to interpret the unmanageability concept in an "all or nothing" manner and get offended by the word. We have all heard tales of Holocaust survivors who have gone on to forge successful careers in medicine, the arts, or other professional areas, but have perhaps developed a drinking problem that gets in the way of interpersonal effectiveness with family and others. It is important to consider that the unmanageability concept may be a hard sell with such individuals because they come into twelve-step recovery feeling a great deal of pride of having been able to rise above their trauma, even if it involved some maladaptive coping (like drinking, using, etc.).

Although it is not directly written into the wording, step one is often described as one of surrender, or raising that proverbial white flag: "I've had enough, the addiction is stronger than me, it wins." For a survivor of trauma, where *flight, fight,* and *freeze* may have crystallized as a way of existence, that *fight* is something that we must be consider. A survivor of trauma may have been defined by *fight* as a mechanism of survival, and so many people in this situation approach their problematic drinking or using behaviors as something that they can *fight*. This logic makes total sense to them because the neurological fight response that was set off at the time of the trauma became a chief mechanism of survival. Once again, surrendering to the power of an addiction may be a solid, ultimate goal for someone who struggles to deal with trauma, but consider that it may be a hard sell at first because it goes against what he has long experienced as familiar.

STEP 2: Came to believe that a Power greater than ourselves could restore us to sanity. Obviously, a great struggle with this step is the element of spirituality it introduces, even for those newcomers to twelve-step programming who do not identify unresolved trauma as a major issue. However, if a trauma survivor relied on the fight of self-sufficiency to get through the trauma and cope over the years, it may be very difficult for her to accept (at first) that something outside of herself is going to help her heal from the addiction. Even if the individual does believe in God and is open to spirituality, reliance on something other than self may be problematic for a trauma survivor. Additionally, the word *sanity* also poses an interesting challenge: if we need to be "restored to sanity," then we must be insane! If a newcomer, especially a trauma survivor, reads this step without having the true meanings of insanity vs. sanity properly explained, there is a greater risk for insult-induced triggering that can happen with some of the slogans we discussed.

STEP 3: Made a decision to turn our will and our lives over to the care of God as *we understood him*. I happen to love the wording of this step because it ushers in a great deal of flexibility for the person to conceptualize God or Higher Power as he sees fit. For so many individuals who grew up in religious institutions with a punishing or an inaccessible God, this step honors a person's individual sense of spirituality. However, the sticking point here for survivors of trauma, regardless of where they stand spiritually, is (once again) this notion of surrender…turning their will over to some outside entity. As discussed in step two, for people who have learned to only rely on themselves or trust only themselves, especially if this learning resulted from a traumatic experience, the idea of "turning it over" may seem impossible, insulting, or too risky.

STEP 4: Made a searching and fearless moral inventory of ourselves.

STEP 5: Admitted to God, to ourselves, and to another human being the exact nature of our wrongs. Steps four and five in a twelve-step program are no doubt the gauntlet for recovering individuals, for these steps ask us to make an inventory of our rights and wrongs (preferably in writing), and then share these findings with another human being. As Nancy explained in chapter 2, doing a fourth and fifth step for an individual with unresolved trauma issues can be a nearly impossible task. For her, and many others, the challenge came in her inability to put her life into proper perspective; reflecting on her past evoked such visceral/body level responses, she found herself unable to cope with the intensity. Individuals with traumatic stress concerns need extra help with these steps, and we discuss these solutions in chapter 6.

In terms of language, many individuals tend to struggle with the word *moral*, especially if they grew up in religious environments, or if they automatically associate the word *immoral* with the idea that they are defective. Once again, they need proper guidance to do this step in a sensitive manner. Another struggle that individuals often have with steps four and five is the entire notion of writing it down and sharing it with someone else. Although we discuss the solutions in the next chapter, consider these legitimate concerns: When she was fourteen years old, one of my former clients decided to journal extensively about the abuse she experienced from her stepfather as a way to try to sort out her feelings. One day, when her mother was cleaning her room, she found the journal and the client was severely "punished" for writing "such slander" about her stepfather. As a result, this client was a little dodgy when it came to writing things down, in fear that the wrong person might find it. I have also dealt with this same struggle with many public safety personnel; past experience had taught many of them that if they were caught with something in writing, they were much more likely to get in trouble for it. Many of the same, potentially irrational but nonetheless valid concerns, exist with the fifth step: What if I get into trouble? What will the person I'm speaking with think of me? What if it gets out? So many individuals who feel that others made them do unspeakably horrible things as the result of their trauma operate with such fear of judgment (real or imagined), that they strive to avoid the fifth step at all costs. Much of this results from a core, trauma-informed belief that they are defective, shameful, or some unique brand of crazy.

A slogan that resounds in the rooms of twelve-step recovery is "If you don't do a fifth (step), you're likely to pick up a fifth (of whiskey)." Sadly, I have seen this to be the case. So many people are scared at the thought of doing a fourth or fifth step, they would rather avoid it, even if that means going back to drinking, using, or engaging in problematic behaviors to avoid really looking at themselves. Indeed, steps four and five are a gauntlet. Often described as the hardest steps to get through, the gauntlet can prove to be especially challenging for those with unresolved trauma...challenging, but not impossible, if proper preparation has taken place. We'll discuss meeting those challenges as we explore solutions in the next chapter.

STEP 6: Were entirely ready to have God remove all these defects of character.

STEP 7: Humbly asked Him to remove our shortcomings.

People often work steps six and seven together, or very closely together, which is why I consider them as a pair in this chapter. Although these steps no doubt come with their share of spiritual challenges, for many, the greatest conceptual challenge of these steps is the idea of *character defects*. In so much of the criticism about twelve-step recovery, many people seem to come back to this idea that twelve-step recovery places too much emphasis on character defects and humility, and not enough emphasis on empowerment.

If a person with unresolved trauma has worked through the first five steps in a properly guided manner, hopefully these steps do not have to be as big of a gauntlet as steps four and five. Nonetheless, if a trauma survivor is still harboring deep-seated negative beliefs about himself such as "I am shameful," "I am worthless," or "I should have done something," the phrase *character defects* can trigger these beliefs and cause a person to get defensive or fall into a greater sense of despair about his selfhood. The word *defect* is what I find to be the potentially problematic sticking point for many survivors, since so many operate with a core belief that "I am defective."

STEP 8: Made a list of all persons we had harmed, and became willing to make amends to them all.

STEP 9: Made direct amends to such people wherever possible, except when to do so would injure them or others.

Steps eight and nine, often referred to as the *making things right* steps, can usher in their own unique set of challenges. Once again, with proper guidance and a productive working through of the previous seven steps, these paired amends steps do not have to be as scary as they seem. However, we must address the common concerns that come up with trauma survivors. I remember that my greatest struggle in working step eight the first time through was a deep sense of anger I had at the fact that some of the people on my list, because I had done some wrong things to them (e.g., stolen money), were some of the same people who had inflicted trauma on me. I argued with my sponsor, "They owe me more of an amends than I owe them!" Such frustrations are common with those in recovery dealing with unresolved trauma. A memorable client from an inpatient facility once told me, as she sat in my office weeping, "I feel that my parents need to be here just as much…maybe even more than I do." Although it may be easy to write this off as a rationalization or excuse, after hearing her story and the abuse she endured for decades, I found myself agreeing with her.

Without proper guidance, working these steps can be a disaster to someone in recovery who has not fully addressed issues of unresolved trauma, especially if people on the *amends list* (step 8) are also some of the same people who inflicted the trauma. If a traumatized individual has not yet taken sufficient steps to reprocess the trauma (either in twelve-step recovery or using other resources like counseling), the likelihood is very high that she will be emotionally ill-equipped to determine what constitutes harm to self or others in making amends. Some of the greatest emotional disasters I have seen with people working steps eight and nine have come from refusing to use the guidance of a sponsor and/or counselor. I have encountered many cases of people in recovery who have gone to abusive parents or an abusive spouse and dumped everything for the sake of making things right, yet the other party clearly does not have the emotional capacity to reason, especially if that other party is still inflicting trauma on others. Thus, further shaming can result from the process of doing steps eight and nine, which is not the intention of the step. *Proper guidance* is a hallmark of the solution chapter that follows. It is important to consider how the lack of proper guidance is a major factor in how working some of these later steps can be retraumatizing.

STEP 10: Continued to take personal inventory and when we were wrong promptly admitted it.

STEP 11: Sought through prayer and meditation to improve our conscious contact with God as we understood Him, praying only for knowledge of His will for us and the power to carry that out.

STEP 12: Having had a spiritual awakening as the result of these steps, we tried to carry this message to alcoholics and to practice these principles in all our affairs.

People often discuss steps ten, eleven, and twelve together as the maintenance steps. In other words, a recovering person has done all of this restoration work in the first nine steps, now it is time to make sure that proper upkeep on the restoration takes place. Of course, steps ten, eleven, and twelve often prove to be a more challenging prospect than simple maintenance, since the steps continue to challenge those who work them with a series of tough tasks...once again, tasks that might prove especially tough for survivors who have not yet worked through the trauma.

Admitting they are wrong is the great challenge of step ten, a task that can be tricky for those easily triggered by traumatic stimuli, who may have a high chance of getting defensive. One of the best places for an individual in early recovery to practice step ten is on the job. I remember in my early recovery, I found it so hard to admit when I was wrong at work because I took every bit of feedback, or every legitimate critique of my performance, as a personal insult. The more I addressed my trauma issues, the less and less I became triggered upon being criticized...and I was thus better able to work step ten on a daily basis.

Step eleven issues what is perhaps one of the greatest spiritual challenges of twelve-step recovery: praying only for knowledge of God's will and the power to carry it out. Many of the struggles trauma survivors face in this step tend to be spiritual in nature. Some people struggle with spirituality in recovery for quite some time, so they may still encounter the same challenges presented by steps two and three with letting go of their self-sufficiency. Yet another dimension has the potential to manifest with this step: the intricacy of God's will. Many trauma survivors have trouble with the concept of God's will, because it may be nearly impossible to wrap their understanding around the notion that the traumatic experiences they endured were somehow God's will. Speaking personally, until I worked through my traumatic stress issues with several reprocessing therapies, I found the *will of God* to be something that was very shady, and as a result, I had great difficulty working step eleven.

In step twelve, the word/concept of *principles* seems to be the sticking point for many. Step twelve challenges those who work it to take the lessons learned in the previous eleven steps and apply them to every facet of their lives. There are several potential difficulties here for trauma survivors, especially if they had to resort to doing certain things that were illegal, immoral, or at the very least unhealthy, to survive the legacy of trauma. Learning a new set of principles, a new way of living, is a shift in perspective. For many survivors of trauma, this includes the difficult process of exchanging the old scripts of existence (which the negative cognitions left by the trauma likely instilled), for a newer, healthier, more principled way of living.

Interestingly, some of the people who seem to have the hardest time with principles of recovery, even if they have worked all twelve steps, are those who continue to struggle with core shame. There are several reasons for this. Shame can often leave people with a message of "You are such a bad person at the core, no matter what you do, you're just going to screw it up anyway, so why bother?" This level of shame typically suggests the presence of unresolved trauma. I have seen people who use their job or their material possessions as a way to somehow prove to the world that they are good enough to be here, when deep down inside they battle a shameful existence. Thus, they end up doing whatever they need to do to keep their job or maintain this material wealth and its accompanied status, even if it involves lying, cheating, manipulating, or other interferences to the principled living that twelve-step recovery suggests.

Meeting Culture: The Problems with Unhealthy Meeting Styles and Sponsorship

All you have to do is go on the Internet to find a host of people who have blogged about, videotaped, or otherwise posted about their negative experiences in Alcoholics Anonymous, other twelve-step fellowships, and even the alternative programs. One of the most common complaints out there is that even though twelve-step fellowships seem to present themselves as welcoming of everyone who has a desire to stop drinking, using, or engaging in any other problematic behaviors that the fellowship strives to address, they quickly become unfriendly, hostile environments if you don't follow the respective recovery program the way they suggest. People who have had negative experiences in recovery programs are often quick to label them "cultish." What is interesting is that the guidelines of the entire AA program, many of the spin-off fellowships, and several of the alternatives are suggestive only. However, something has happened in the way that meetings are set up and in the manner in which people conduct themselves at meetings that can allow recovery programs to project this cultish, *our way or the highway* mentality.

I know, as a personal advocate of twelve-step programs, it is easy to read these critics of twelve-step recovery and write them off as people who are resistant, or who sport a large chip on their shoulder because they couldn't follow the suggestions of a twelve-step program. However, as a professional, I can't help but acknowledge that some of these critics have a point—not everyone who walks through the doors of recovery group has a positive experience. In my practice, clients have shared with me a variety of experiences, everything from going to a first meeting and feeling preached at or belittled, to experiences as horrible as being raped in the parking lot following a meeting by a member of a recovery fellowship. We are turning a blind eye and living in ignorance if we choose to ignore that such things can, and do happen. Moreover, I have heard a multitude of stories from my patients and clients about negative experiences with sponsorship, ranging from militaristic sponsors who use belittling tactics, to unethical sponsors who ended up cheating with the wives of sponsees. As much as those of us in recovery programs may not want to hear about these experiences, *knowing that they don't represent what recovery programs mean to promote,* we must acknowledge that such experiences have caused some people to write off recovery programs completely.

The purpose of this section is not to address all of these criticisms of twelve-step or traditional recovery, nor is it to referee the debate in any way. However, since this book is meant to promote trauma sensitivity in working recovery principles with clients and sponsees, I assert that we must keep two words in mind—*flexibility* and *safety.* The best way to look at flexibility in a trauma-sensitive context is that it represents the ability to meet a newcomer where he or she is *at* in the recovery or change process. Flexibility is the opposite of rigidity, and rigidity is a trait that is on display in so many recovery meetings and at so many treatment centers. Rigidity manifests itself in a variety of ways in meetings, usually as absolute letter-of-the-law adherence to the twelve traditions (which are, like the steps, meant to be suggestive only). One of the most disturbing ways that I see rigidity in practice at meetings is when home group members at certain meetings get absolutely fundamentalist about the fact that you can only talk about alcohol at Alcoholics Anonymous meetings, or that you can only talk about narcotics at Narcotics Anonymous meetings. God forbid, if you are at an Alcoholics Anonymous meeting and happen to mention how drugs relate to your story, or if you should mention the role that trauma or mental health concerns played in your addiction, you may be subjecting yourself to a public scolding by home-group members.

Fortunately, not all meetings are created equally, and there are some that display more tolerance (and, in my opinion, realism) when it comes to flexibility about sharing on other addictions or problems, as they relate to the primary focus of the fellowship. However, imagine that you are an individual going to your first meeting. Your defenses are already up, not only because of the addiction, but also because of your legacy of trauma. When you speak to someone at the meeting and mention that you're addicted to pills and alcohol and they gruffly cut you off with, "We don't talk about drugs here, just alcohol," that sends a message that *you're not welcome here unless you do it our way.*

This *my way or the highway* mentality tends to manifest itself in sponsorship styles as well. Many recovering folks jokingly call twelve-step sponsors "AA Nazis" or "Big Book Thumpers" because they are so rigid to the letter of the law/book and may not even consider sponsoring you unless you take all of their suggestions, their way, period. Now, I don't want to make a blanket criticism of such sponsors, because certain people in recovery programs respond well to this style. However, I would argue that most newcomers who come to recovery fellowships with unresolved trauma more often experience harm than help, especially in the long run, by such an approach. I remember something that my own twelve-step sponsor, who now has thirty years of recovery, once shared with me. She told me that when she first came to a twelve-step fellowship, she asked a woman to sponsor her, and the woman responded that she would only agree to it if "you do everything my way…if not, then I'm not your sponsor." As my sponsor then shared, "I couldn't do it…it felt too much like home." For my sponsor, and for many of us who have struggled with trauma concerns, something that feels too much like home is not synonymous with healthy recovery.

Now, I am not advocating that we have to be goody-goody and treat all newcomers who have had horrible pasts with white kid gloves. However, we must remember that twelve-step recovery is meant to be suggestive only, and we ought to deliver our help to others in that spirit of making suggestions based on our experience, strength, and hope. We should not be using our roles as recovery sponsors (or counselors who operate from a twelve-step paradigm) as a way to get our needs of being in charge met! Even if you feel like you are being an "AA Nazi" or "Big Book Thumper" because tough love worked for you, don't assume that it will work for everyone. Yes, some people may respond well to it, but most who have unresolved trauma concerns will likely not feel safe with that style.

Safety is the other key element that we must consider in looking at trauma-sensitive recovery. In meetings, in our sponsorship style, in our treatment centers, and in our support circles, are we doing all we can to make sure that newcomers feel safe? I do not believe a person can meaningfully recover until he or she feels safe to do so, yet so many people come to meetings where they do not feel safe. Even though it is unrealistic to expect a perfect sense of safety at every twelve-step recovery meeting, some simple things that might promote it often go unnoticed. For one, I have absolutely no place for the public shaming that so often goes on in many recovery meetings, be they twelve-step or alternative meetings. Allow me to share a case of one of my former clients.

Brandalyn found herself in treatment for the first time. Even though she had sensed for some time that she had a problem with alcohol and sleeping pills, she was ultimately court ordered to treatment for possession of crack cocaine—a substance she had only began using one year prior to her arrest. A strong-willed woman with an extensive history of childhood sexual abuse, she was initially scared off from going to AA meetings because someone had told her that "drug addicts weren't welcome," even though alcohol was her first drug of choice. Thus, Brandalyn decided to attend NA meetings, and she had a pretty good experience, feeling optimistic about her membership in that fellowship following two weeks of attendance. Then, at an NA discussion meeting, she decided to end her share with a poem that her treatment counselor had given about the power of surrender, unaware that you are not supposed to share materials that aren't *conference-approved literature* (a term that meant nothing to her as a newcomer) at an NA meeting. An NA member literally tore into her, not even letting her finish her share, telling her that the poem she read was not a part of the NA program and thus it had no business at an NA meeting. Upon hearing him scream at her, she panicked, and the old feeling of being scolded for doing something that she had no idea was "wrong" came flooding back. Even though the member was technically correct, what he *should* have done (preferably with another female member of the fellowship), was approach Brandalyn after the meeting and explain to her the difference between conference-approved literature and general recovery literature, noting that conference-approved literature is all that gets shared within the meeting itself.

Brandalyn came back to treatment flustered, feeling unwelcome and unsafe in both AA and NA because of the experiences that happened in both fellowships. Fortunately, Brandalyn was able to keep an open mind in treatment for a couple more weeks, and when she was feeling stronger, she agreed to try some new AA and NA meetings to see if her experience would be different elsewhere. Fortunately, it was, and Brandalyn was able to work through her steps. One of the key factors that helped Brandalyn stick with twelve-step recovery was seeking out an encouraging support team, with the help of her counselor, who understood the uniqueness of her situation as a cross-addicted female with issues of unresolved childhood sexual trauma. To this day, I believe that if Brandalyn had not found the sponsor and cosponsor that she did— women with solid recovery who were able to meet Brandalyn where she was *at* in her recovery process and gently explain the steps and traditions to her—she never would have stuck with a twelve-step recovery program.

Solid sponsorship can make all the difference between whether or not a person, especially a traumatized person, sticks around and gives a recovery program a chance to work. Sponsors who publicly shame or are dictatorial in their styles, as we've discussed throughout this section, can prove to be problematic. Another major area of offense that happens a lot in twelve-step recovery fellowships, an offense that clearly violates the notion of safety, is when sponsors attempt to work too far outside their scope of experience. Many times, sponsors attempt to play counselor to clients about matters that would be more appropriately handled by a professional (and the AA Big Book does acknowledge that sometimes outside help is needed). More dangerously, they will advise a person with mental health concerns to go off of his or her psychotropic medications because all they need is to work the twelve steps. Personally and professionally, I have no patience for this, and I have seen this attitude cause more harm than good to countless people who have taken this advice literally.

Some people in twelve-step recovery programs will read this chapter and think I am complicating matters. One of the biggest criticisms I expect to receive is that Alcoholics Anonymous is just about alcohol, Narcotics Anonymous is just about narcotics, Cocaine Anonymous is just about cocaine, Overeaters Anonymous is just about overeating, etc., and that twelve-step recovery fellowships are not designed to deal with other issues like trauma complications or mental health. I agree with that statement to a certain extent. In their purest form, the design of these fellowships is not to address the plethora of issues people may deal with; however, the reality is that most newcomers entering the rooms of twelve-step recovery today are coming in with a plethora of issues. Look back to the statistics presented in chapter 3 about how significant the comorbidity is between PTSD and substance dependence. If we turn a blind eye to these other issues and stay rigid just for the sake of tradition (or whatever unmet ego needs of ours we're trying to satisfy), we will be alienating a whole new generation of people, especially people with serious trauma wounds, who can benefit from what recovery programs can provide. In the coming chapter, I hope to tie together all that we have discussed so far and spell out specific ideas for how we can put trauma-sensitive, twelve-step recovery in action, whether we are professionals or members of twelve-step fellowships ourselves.

Toolkit Strategy: Honoring the Experience of the Person

Looking back on your time in working with others, what are some of the greatest "horror stories" you have heard from your clients or sponsees about negative experiences they had in recovery meetings or treatment groups? If you'd like, take a few minutes to jot some of those down. Then consider how you, as a professional or sponsor, addressed these concerns when the person brought them to your attention. Looking back on it now, would you have done anything differently?

CHAPTER 6

Working with Others in a Trauma-Sensitive Manner

My first sponsor, Janet, was a gem. She exemplified the art of being able to meet me, an addicted woman with a plethora of trauma issues, where I was *at* during my early days in recovery. I was resistant, bull-headed, and prideful despite my obvious outreach to her for help, but there were so many things she did that, I believe, set a good example of what recovery could offer. In my work as a professional today, I get so disheartened when I hear people share about negative experiences with addiction recovery programs, thinking to myself, "If only you could have had someone like Janet..."

Janet did not get hung up on whether I chose to identify myself as an alcoholic or addict. When I first sought out recovery, I had no problem admitting that I was an addict, but I couldn't quite accept that I was an alcoholic. In the Bosnian town where I was living at the time, there were only AA meetings. She told me to come to the meetings and if I heard the word *alcohol*, just replace it with *drugs*..."it's all gonna kill you anyway," she told me in her pronounced, Kentucky drawl. This simple action made such an impression on me because it told me that I did not have to force myself to identify or fit in. By her not preaching to me from the onset, I was able to go to meetings with an open mind, and it eventually clicked in my stubborn brain that I was both a drug addict and an alcoholic.

Another powerful way that Janet helped to meet me where I was at on the road to recovery was by demonstrating a clear understanding of my past and how it affected me. One time, something my boss said to me made me cry so hard, almost to the point of convulsing, and Janet said simply, "This just isn't tears, Jamie, this is a post-traumatic reaction." This was such a simple validation, but it allowed me to feel safe with her in exploring why my boss's behavior so deeply affected me. Janet did not let me sit in self-pity; however, she exemplified the art of first validating, then challenging me to action. Her classic line was, "Jamie, after everything you've been through, no wonder you're feeling this way…but what are you going to do about it now?" The sensitive combination of acceptance and challenge helped me work through my issue of both addiction recovery and unresolved trauma in those early days when hearing one wrong thing could have turned me off to recovery forever.

Like many a newcomer to recovery and supportive fellowships, I challenged Janet on just about everything I heard. "What do you mean, I'm powerless?" I would taunt as she strove to explain the first step to me, "I spent years taking care of myself emotionally…not to mention I'm an overachiever and I always succeed when I put my mind to something." Once again, she validated my concerns in an appropriate manner, not making me feel stupid for bringing up the objection, and then asked me to consider another spin on the concept of *powerlessness*. I also challenged Janet about the importance of meetings (and going to so many of them), why she felt it was necessary for me to stay out of a romantic relationship, and why I had to change every aspect of my lifestyle if I was going to stay sober long term. Janet didn't spoon-feed me recovery; she let me hit some road bumps along the way and reminded me that she was there for me when I was ready. And after a year of trial and error, when I finally took my last drink and became ready to take suggestions, I knew she would be the one to help me, so positive was the impression that she left on me in the craziness of early sobriety.

So much of what made Janet an exemplary recovery sponsor was that in her professional life, she had been a social worker and chemical dependency counselor. Thus, she was knowledgeable about what the fields of psychology, science, and medicine have learned about addiction. This knowledge meant she understood the realities of traumatic stress and how it can get in the way of learning new ways of living and embracing recovery. Her knowledge about addiction as a brain disease and the phenomena of cravings also informed her that it's futile to get hung up on one specific drug as a prerequisite to attend and to benefit from meetings. At the level of the brain, addiction is addiction, and acceptance of people with cross-addiction issues is absolutely vital in all forms of recovery meetings today.

You do not have to be a social worker or drug and alcohol counselor to be an exemplary twelve-step sponsor or mentor/leader in another type of recovery program. Sadly, I have seen many social workers, counselors, and drug and alcohol professionals who still choose to operate with the same rigidity of certain twelve-step sponsors who meet newcomers with an *it's my way or the highway* attitude. The message in this chapter is that to be a trauma-sensitive professional or sponsor/recovery program leader, you need to honor certain principles: safety and flexibility. Embrace the phrase *meet them where they're at*…let this phrase guide you. This phrase is so important if we are going to make trauma-informed addiction care a reality. Meeting people where they are *at* is a principle so many professionals and sponsors like Janet already practice. However, the logic of it still needs to be more widely practiced in modern recovery so that traumatized people are not alienated as a result of being retraumatized by rigid professionals, sponsors, or community members.

In this chapter, we explore how honoring the ideas of safety and flexibility are the most important feature of working with others in a trauma-sensitive manner. I explain the importance of safety to a traumatized person and share best practices for helping a person feel safe. Then we will explore how using the stages of change model (Prochaska, Norcross, & DiClemente, 1994), which is widely used in the addiction treatment field, can help all of us better understand how to work with others in a flexible manner. Finally, we discuss some of the language problems with the twelve steps and some time-honored recovery slogans uncovered in chapter 5 and how you can help to address reactions that traumatized newcomers may have upon encountering these difficulties. In this section, we'll learn that the best answer to newcomers' struggles with recovery may be to stop the *recoveryspeak* and simply validate their concerns.

Safety

People with unresolved trauma issues tend to live life on full alert…one commonly held belief is *I am not safe in the world*. Sometimes, trauma survivors try to function while battling the belief of *I am not safe with myself*. Moreover, the very prospect of change could seem unsafe: meetings, therapy, reaching out to people, and the process of self-exploration are risks, and making a decision to take these risks can be scary. Thus, as people who are in a position to help newcomers affected by trauma, we must recognize how important it is to create an environment that is as safe as possible for the change process to take place. When an individual affected by trauma does not feel safe, his tendency is to run, and we must recognize this connection as a potential reason why traumatized newcomers do not stay around long enough to give recovery a full chance to work.

Professionals who treat PTSD and other trauma-related issues consistently agree that establishing a sense of safety and stabilization is the necessary first stage of treatment (for reviews, see Curran, 2010; Marich, 2011). Let's take a look at what some of the world's leading experts on traumatic stress have to say about the importance of safety in the treatment of traumatic stress concerns:

- "Because trauma is about vulnerability to danger, safety is a crucial issue for trauma survivors. It is often only in perceived safe environments that those who have been exposed to danger can let down their guard and experience the relative luxury of introspection and connection. In therapy, safety involves, at minimum, the absence of physical danger, psychological maltreatment, exploitation, or rejection" (Briere & Scott, 2006; p.71).

- "Psychological safety…means that the client will not perceive himself or herself to be criticized, humiliated, rejected, dramatically misunderstood, needlessly interrupted, or laughed at during the treatment process" (Briere & Scott, 2006; p.71).

- "The feeling of safety, fostered by the bond with a trusted companion, counteracts fear (alarm/anxiety), promotes exploration and risk-taking, and fosters a full affective experience. If there is no feeling of safety, anxiety, the mother of all psychopathology, takes hold" (Fosha, 2000; p. 47).

- "When the threat of recurrence of a trauma persists, the first step is to negotiate how the patient can achieve a greater sense of safety. When it appears that the risk of further traumatization has ended, there may still be residual vulnerability if the traumatic circumstances should return. A supportive approach, including personal validation through acknowledging the reality of symptoms, is often of considerable help; the mere opportunity to disclose to another human being some part of one's experience can be enormously comforting" (Turner, McFarlane, & van der Kolk, 1994; p. 546).

- "*Safety*, rapport, *safety*, trust, and *safety* are of such critical importance that it can't be overstated" (Curran, 2010; p.33).

- "The intensity of the shame and guilt that often pervades much of a survivor's internal experience makes it that much harder to expose herself to others. Clients who can safely engage with a clinician or with a therapy group report profound gratitude and exhibit greater treatment progress" (Hien, Litt, Cohen, Miele, & Campbell, 2009; p. 89).

Although these passages target counselors and professionals, they all convey a general wisdom that those who work with addicted individuals can embrace.

Certain best practices will help to ensure the safety of the people you work with. Following these best practices will ensure that you are on the right track in providing as safe an environment as possible for healing to occur:

- **Do *not* retraumatize.** Sometimes, well-intentioned professionals and sponsors retraumatize without even realizing that we are doing it. This tends to occur when we pressure people for too much detail about the nature of their traumatic experience before they are ready to give it, particularly if we act like interrogators or pressure them to "get it all out," especially in meetings or group where they may feel unsafe or unready. Retraumatization also occurs when we invalidate a person's experience by making comments such as, "You need to show some gratitude, there's always someone out there who has it worse." Even though that gratitude-based statement may be true and may eventually serve as a solution, bluntly saying it to a person without first validating the experience can open an old wound. Militaristic or dictatorial styles in sponsorship or counseling may also be part of the retraumatization culprit.

- **Do consider the role of shame in both addiction and trauma.** Shame is that essential belief that, at my core, I am a bad person. An often-made distinction is that guilt is feeling bad about things you have *done*, but shame is feeling bad about who you *are*. The vast majority of people seeking treatment for addiction have profound shame, and the complexity of this shame compounds if we add negative beliefs resulting from trauma into a person's cognitive mix. The toxicity of unaddressed shame is a major factor in why some of what may seem like our most helpful comments can come across as retraumatizing.

- **Do be nonjudgmental.** Being nonjudgmental does not mean that we should endorse bad or negative behavior. However, it does mean that we ought to refrain from name-calling, or other shaming, "hot seat" techniques that sometimes occur in addiction treatment centers or twelve-step meetings. We can call out or challenge the behaviors while always respecting the dignity of the person.

- **Do be genuine as you build rapport.** Respecting the dignity of a person does not mean that you have to be fake, phony, or saccharine. Addicted people and survivors of trauma can pick up on a fake person a mile away! When I train professionals, I convey this suggestion as *be the best version of yourself possible.*

- **Ask open-ended questions.** Although this is a suggestion typically given to professionals, sponsors can benefit from it as well. An open-ended question cannot be answered with a simple "yes or no." Moreover, open-ended questions typically avoid the word *why*, since the answer we tend to get with *why* questions is "I don't know," and if a person genuinely doesn't know what compels her to engage in a certain destructive behavior, being asked why can come across as more shaming. Solid, open-ended questions typically begin with the words *what* or *how.* Examples include, "What were things like for you growing up?" or "How did that affect you?" Such questions invite a new client or sponsee to give you as much or as little detail as he is ready to give at any given point.

- **Do convey experience, strength, and hope.** In twelve-step circles, giving directives to people is not encouraged, but sharing experience, strength, and hope is. Following this suggestion is massively important in conveying safety. A trauma survivor is so much more likely to feel safe with us if we refrain from telling her what to do (unless she asks for direct suggestions). We should convey a sense—based on our experiences—that hope for recovery is possible. We must be careful not to minimize in using this strategy; for example, avoid saying things like, "Well, everyone in this room has been through that, you'll get through it." However, first honoring the struggle and then conveying the hope can work wonders.

- **Do have closure strategies ready.** This is another best practice that I often convey in training counselors, but it is one that sponsors can adhere to as well. Bar none, one of the greatest errors I see in trauma treatment is letting the person leave a session while he is still activated, anxious, or jumpy. Ending a session—a one-on-one meeting with a sponsee or a telephone call—hastily with a person who has not calmed down fully may put that person at risk for engaging in a self-destructive behavior. At the end of a challenging session or phone call we can bring the conversation back to lighter, more general banter, or suggest that the person take some breaths or engage in some body-based action (e.g., go outside and take a walk, get into a hot bath, go and pick up your kids like you committed to). Using these strategies, we are helping bring them out of an emotional, potentially destructive place. We will cover this further in chapter 7.

Flexibility and the Stages of Change

Prochaska & DiClemente's *stages of change* model is often used in the addiction treatment field to conceptualize cases, and many counselors even teach this model to people so that clients can get a better sense of where they are *at* in their change processes. The stages are:

- *Precontemplation:* The person is not prepared to take any action at this time or in the foreseeable future.

- *Contemplation:* The person is intending to change soon.

- *Preparation:* The person is intending to make a change in the immediate future.

- *Action:* The person is making significant changes in his or her lifestyle.

- *Maintenance:* The person is working to prevent relapse.

- *Termination:* The person has achieved 100 percent self-efficacy, and the relapse potential is near zero. (Of course, most followers of twelve-step philosophy argue that a recovering addict is *always* in maintenance, and that stage six is not relevant. However, this stage is relevant to other approaches to addiction recovery.)

Perhaps more important than teaching the stages of change to clients is that we as helpers, either professionals or sponsors, use the model to help us see where each individual is *at* in her change process. One of the most counterproductive approaches we can take, for instance, is to bombard a person who is precontemplative with a series of action-oriented interventions, like *Go to ninety meetings in ninety days,* or, *It's time to start working your steps.* In the following table, we take a look at each stage of change, characteristics of people in that stage of change, and approaches that are best for working with people, especially addicted survivors of trauma, at each stage.

Stage of Change	Commonly Encountered Attitudes About Recovery	Suggested Approaches
Precontemplation	"I don't have a problem, but other people say I do."	-supportive listening -invite to attend a meeting or support group just to "check it out"
Contemplation	"I'm thinking that it might be a good idea if I cut back my drinking, I'm starting to get too depressed."	-supportive listening -invite to check out a meeting or support group, explain how meetings can benefit
Preparation	"Well, what my counselor is saying and what I'm hearing at the meetings is making sense; I just don't know if I'm ready to really commit to changing."	-supportive listening with sharing of experience, strength, and hope if listener is receptive -make the suggestion for more regular meeting attendance and getting to know more people in recovery

Action	"I've gotta stop...I'm ready to take suggestions and listen."	-make the suggestion for regular meetings (typically ninety meetings in the first ninety days is suggested, but a minimum of three to four a week may be sufficient depending on the person) -make the suggestion to begin step work with the guidance of a sponsor -advise building a support group
Maintenance	"Recovery has to be a way of life for me."	-as a sponsor or a support figure, work out a plan with the person to determine number of meetings, best possible recovery tools, and, if needed, outside help for long-term wellness
Termination	"I don't have a problem with drinking or drugs anymore, it's all in the past."	-supportive listening -ask about quality of life, and, if appropriate, suggest that checking out some meetings again or connecting with others in recovery may enhance wellness

This table is not exhaustive, yet it can serve as a general guide to the nature of our approach in working with newcomers. People who are new to recovery, especially those who are still jumpy around anything different due to the residual effects of trauma, need to be worked with in a flexible manner while they determine if recovery, specifically recovery groups and people, are safe for them. Honoring their needs for safety and flexibility will have a positive impact on retention in the long run. An often-intoned recovery slogan shared with newcomers is "Don't leave before the miracle happens." However, we must consider that our behaviors can impact whether or not a person sticks around.

Addressing the Language Problems with Slogans and Steps

Comprehending the language of recovery can be a difficult task for any newcomer, especially a newcomer who has had extensive experience with language as a means of wounding. Think about verbal or emotional abuse survivors in particular—the least little saying delivered in the wrong tone can trigger a profound reaction. Now, this is not to say that those of us in positions of guidance need to mind every little word we say with newcomers; that wouldn't be realistic. But there are two points to consider. When sharing new knowledge like slogans and steps with people first coming into recovery programs, pay attention to your delivery and tone. Review some of the best practices listed earlier in the chapter for tips on being nonjudgmental and genuine. From my experience working with clients, so many trauma survivors are alienated from twelve-step meetings or other support groups because people came across to them as "know-it-alls" or they felt as though others were talking down to them.

The other major point to keep in mind is that resistance to new knowledge is completely normal for someone who is going through the lifestyle changes required for recovery. Thus, a person emotionally reacting to a certain slogan or step is not necessarily a negative development, nor does it mean that recovery and the people who are a part of recovery groups have failed them. What it does mean is that a newcomer will need support and validation through this reaction, and then if the person is open to it, a sponsor or counselor can explain the intention of the slogan and entertain some dialogue.

The key is to validate (addressing the emotional or limbic brain) before appealing to reason (the neocortex or rational brain). Let's take the slogan "You're only as sick as your secrets" as an example. Although twelve-step recovery circles often use this slogan, other approaches and models use it as well. Here is a sample dialogue that demonstrates how a professional or a counselor may best address the traumatized newcomer's reaction to the slogan:

Newcomer: I'm not too crazy about something that some old lady told me at the Wednesday afternoon discussion meeting. I was talking about how hard it was for me to even come to these meetings because of all this shame I have about my past, and she said, in a real nasty way, "You're only as sick as your secrets."

Sponsor/Counselor: Oh, dear.

Newcomer: That really pissed me off.

Sponsor/Counselor: Well, I can certainly see why it would.

Newcomer: I mean, she doesn't know me at all.

Sponsor/Counselor: Well, can you tell me what upset you so much about hearing that?

Newcomer: Yeah, it's like, who the heck is she to say something like that—she doesn't know me. She doesn't know that if I didn't keep all those things that my stepfather did to us secret, our mother would have put us out.

Sponsor/Counselor: So, for you, keeping secrets really was a matter of survival.

Newcomer: Well, yeah.

Sponsor/Counselor: So I can definitely see now why hearing that slogan upset you so much.

Newcomer: It's like she was calling me sick for doing what I had to do.

Sponsor/Counselor: Well, yeah. Was there anything else about the meeting that bothered you?

Newcomer: Not really.

Sponsor/Counselor: Ok. Well, I definitely think what that lady at the meeting did to you was not cool, just saying the slogan like that in front of the whole meeting without really knowing you. However, "You're only as sick as your secrets" does have some value as it applies to recovery...are you willing to let me explain?

Newcomer: Sure.

Sponsor/Counselor: Well, "You're only as sick as your secrets" doesn't mean that you have to spill your guts to everyone about your past. But it does mean that all of those things you've been holding in over the years have kept you stuck—maybe *stuck* is a better word than *sick*—and will eventually need to come out in order for you to move forward in your recovery and feel better about yourself. But only when you're ready, and only with the people who you deem trustworthy.

Newcomer: Hmm...well, that makes a lot more sense. I don't think I would have overreacted so much if she had explained it that way. Can we talk about what I need to do to get ready?

Sponsor/Counselor: Absolutely.

Although not all conversations will go this smoothly, this is a general guideline of how first validating can lead to more productive conversations for reasoning. This method can work with just about any problem a newcomer has with a slogan or language in step: validate, then explain...and then you will typically find that the newcomer is open to further exploration. Proper guidance delivered in the spirit of meeting a newcomer where he or she is *at* in his or her recovery and in the stages of change is absolutely vital.

Let's take a look at another example of a potential problem area that a newcomer with a history of trauma may experience, this time using one of the steps:

Newcomer: Powerless. I hate that word *powerless.*

Sponsor/Counselor: Well, what do you hate about it?

Newcomer: I don't know...it's like saying that I'm giving up, and I'm not the kind of person to quit.

Sponsor/Counselor: Well, knowing what I know about your history, you're definitely not a quitter, you're a survivor.

Newcomer: So I don't like admitting that I'm powerless.

Sponsor/Counselor: Well, can I make a suggestion that might help?

Newcomer: Sure.

Sponsor/Counselor: The step just asks us to admit that we're powerless over *alcohol*, not that we're powerless people.

Newcomer: What's the difference?

Sponsor/Counselor: Well, admitting that we're powerless over alcohol, or whatever the drug may be, is simply admitting that when we drink or use, our lives go to hell. The alcohol and the drugs will always win. That's all the step is saying. It doesn't say that we're powerless people. Actually, it kind of gives us a way to take our power back.

Newcomer: What do you mean? Isn't that a contradiction?

Sponsor/Counselor: Well, you're right, it does seem like an oxymoron, and I had the same struggle when I came into recovery. But I learned that in admitting that the alcohol would always win and not even trying to fight that fight, the real power inside of me—the power I had to survive and to make good decisions—was able to come through.

Newcomer: Well, I still don't know if I fully understand it, but the way you explained it makes a lot more sense.

You can address all the language problems that newcomers may encounter in the twelve steps or other recovery approaches using this method of *validate-explain-discuss*. Of course, you'll need to account for individual differences in experience and temperament, and the more effectively you're able to do that, the more effectively you'll be able to work with the newcomer. If a person is having a hard time connecting with the 1930s language of the book *Alcoholics Anonymous* or other texts, consider having her look at other books that may cover the sample principles in modern language. Take a look at some of the website recommendations in chapter 4.

A vital aspect of trauma-sensitive recovery is acknowledging that no recovery program means to be a panacea, or cure-all. So often, people new to recovery encounter this attitude from others, even counselors in traditional treatment programs, and it's unfortunate. Comments like, "You don't need those psych meds, all you need are the twelve steps of recovery," or "You're complicating it by going to all of those shrinks; you gotta keep it simple and work the program" (whatever program that may be), or "You just need to go to church and our group for addicts" abound. Even though self-help groups and the members of them are not bound to professional ethics, it is truly troubling to hear that such attitudes are common in recovery groups. Whether the people who make these comments realize it or not, they are actually doing more harm than good to the reputation of recovery programs—twelve-step or others—in the community (see "The Case of Beth"). Moreover, they are going against the guidance that Bill Wilson himself made in writing *Alcoholics Anonymous,* in which he stressed the value of outside help and guidance.

Sometimes, the best approach you can take in working with a person struggling with recovery is to put down the *recoveryspeak*—the slogans, steps, and therapeutic clichés that abound in meetings and treatment literature. So often, a person just needs a human connection when in distress and doesn't need to have solutions thrown at him immediately. Consider this sharing from author Kiera Van Gelder (2010), a woman with nine years of sobriety in Narcotics Anonymous who found herself on disability for unmanageable mental illness, including borderline personality disorder:

> *"[My father has] been sober eleven years, and I've just passed my ninth. Although his support as a father was minimal, at least we now share some understanding about addiction. Whenever I'm in pain, falling apart, or in crisis, he gives me slogans: Easy does it. First things first. Keep it simple. Ask your higher power for help. Go to a meeting. If I were to call him and tell him I've just split up with Bennet, I doubt I'd get sympathy. He'd probably just suggest I do another moral inventory. F*&% moral inventories."* (p. 34)

Although a twelve-step purist may read Kiera's words and accuse her of being resistant, we have to take her perspective into consideration, because it reflects the views of so many who struggle with both trauma and addiction recovery. In chapter 8, we discuss in depth the healing elements of the relationship and explore the idea that *how* you say things to newcomers and clients is so much more important than *what* you say.

The Case of Beth

Beth sought out services at a local counseling agency where a therapist specialized in the integrated treatment of trauma in addicted women. Eager to work on some issues related to her past, Beth's counselor did a preliminary screening of her safety needs and asked if she was going to meetings and had a sponsor. Beth replied, "Well, I'm doing about eight meetings a week. There aren't too many sober women in my town, and I asked the one with the most sobriety to sponsor me. But every time we talk, she always brings it back to how I shouldn't be on so many psych meds. We haven't even gotten to any steps yet because that's all she wants to talk about."

After a few preliminary sessions, Beth and her counselor mutually concluded that it would be best for her if she sought out a new sponsor. Beth's psychiatric symptoms, which included a long history of PTSD and suicide attempts, were stable, and the psychotropic medications she was taking for maintenance were not addictive. When Beth found a sponsor who understood mental illness and didn't always insist on bringing their discussion back to her medications, Beth was able to work the steps and obtain the support she needed. Both activities helped her more fully invest in the counseling process; eventually, her PTSD symptoms went into remission, her suicidal ideations totally disappeared, and with a year of sobriety, she began attending college.

For Twelve-Step Sponsors

If you are a sponsor and a newcomer with trauma concerns is not connecting after you make attempts at this style of guidance, it may be a sign that what *Alcoholics Anonymous* calls "outside help" may be needed (Alcoholics Anonymous World Services, 2001). Depending on a person's needs, outside help can refer to seeking out a counselor, clinical social worker, psychologist, psychiatrist, pastoral counselor, minister, or alternative healthcare provider (e.g., acupuncturist, massage therapist/bodywork specialist). Alcoholics Anonymous and the other fellowships I am aware of endorse the use of outside help when warranted. Newcomers with traumatic stress concerns may benefit from outside help at various points in early recovery, especially if they are struggling with fourth and fifth step work. But seeking outside help with twelve-step recovery is not just for the newcomer. People with years in recovery often seek outside help from professionals if too many issues surface that the twelve steps cannot address in isolation, affecting quality of life.

Toolkit Strategy: The Stages of Change

If you are currently working with clients that have both addiction and trauma concerns, or if you are presently sponsoring recovering individuals in some type of recovery group, take a few moments and jot down the names or initials of those individuals. Then, going through the list, evaluate where each person is "at" in the stages of change model. Consider whether how you have been approaching or working with that individual is appropriate for where he or she is at in the stages of change. If not, how can you modify your approach?

CHAPTER 7

Bring Your Butt, The Rest Will Follow —The Importance of Honoring the Body in Addiction Recovery

One day, Janet declared in her thick, memorable accent, "Remember, Jamie, chapter 6 of the (AA) Big Book is called *Into Action*, not *Into Thinking*." She then proceeded to share with me another recovery saying: "It's easier to act your way into better thinking than to think your way into better acting," and she reminded me that if people are unable to go through the motions of action with sincerity, then just "Fake it 'til you make it." Others use such sayings in response to people in recovery who get hung up on the thinking aspect of their problems. Another great one is "Too much analysis leads to paralysis." What many people in recovery programs may not realize is that such action-oriented slogans are very trauma-sensitive.

Remember what we covered in chapter 3—the triune brain is essentially three brains working as one: the reptilian (survival) brain, the limbic (emotional) brain, and the neocortical (rational) brain. If you recall, when the survival and emotional brain are in the metaphorical driver's seat (which typically happens when some outside stimulus triggers a person), the rational brain shuts down. Although the rational brain is what makes us uniquely human, it is also the most complex of the three brains to access. Hence, we can think about, talk about, and analyze a problem until we are blue in the face, but unless we access those lower regions of the brain as well, it is hard for the new information to truly integrate into the brain, or "sink in." Interventions are always best if they start at the lower regions of the brain and work up. Interestingly, activating those lower regions of the brain is not as hard as it seems—those lower regions are the *action* parts of the brain. The higher, neocortical region is the *thinking* part of the brain.

Let's look at a pure recovery example to further illuminate this point. One of the classic recovery tools is using the phone. If clients feel triggered, tempted, or otherwise overwhelmed, advise them to call their sponsor or other members of their support group. Although many people in these situations report that talking to someone in recovery can be a lifesaver, the primary action at work is not the *talking through*. To call their sponsor or another support figure, they first need to pick up the phone—a clear action step. Then, they need to dial the numbers—another action step. Once the person answers the phone, a connection occurs; if that connection is with a sponsor they've developed a good relationship with, then they can often experience a calming response whether or not either of them speaks a word—this relational connection is actually a lower-level brain function as well. If their sponsor allows them to vent and then provides validation, this is also a process that has very little to do with the rational brain. Thus, even if the conversation does reveal excellent, rational insight for the clients doing the calling, several action steps took place first that allowed their brains to be more open to rational guidance and reasoning.

Using the rational brain to cope is not all negative. In fact, it is a fantastic, ultimate goal for people in recovery from both trauma and addiction to begin operating more with their rational minds and less with their emotional minds. However, true recovery requires integrating the two, and this best happens by using the lower regions of the brain as an access point. Put simply, take the action first, and the thoughts and words will follow. In my professional experience, the best trauma therapies utilize this logic, and this logic can blend elegantly with many of the tools and philosophies of traditional recovery. In this chapter, we take a deeper look at the elements of the twelve-step and traditional recovery philosophies that already take this action-oriented approach to heart. Then we look at simple, body-based strategies from the psychotherapeutic and other healing professions such as breathing, muscle relaxation, and mindfulness that people can easily pick up to enhance their daily recovery programs. Such body-based strategies may prove essential to those with trauma issues who may have a difficult time sitting still in meetings or tolerating the intense emotion that comes along with step work.

Into Action, Not Into Thinking

The physical steps required to pick up a telephone and reach out are classic examples of action-based steps that can aid in recovery. Several other examples of action-based steps that tools of traditional recovery promote may prove especially useful to the recovering person with unresolved trauma. We already covered how use of the telephone is an excellent, action-based step. Let's take a look at some others.

Going to meetings. Many people report that in the early days of recovery, not much from the meetings really "sank in"; however, the mere action of having to be somewhere, interact with others, and sit still for an hour or so was a form of therapy in and of itself. Sometimes when I go to a meeting, I don't get much out of it—I don't connect with the speaker or I don't have much to contribute to the discussion. However, the act of committing to sit still for an hour is me practicing, or putting into action, the skills of patience and self-care. Thus, I can honestly say that I take something out of every meeting, even if it is this practice of sitting through the meeting. Once again, it is taking the actions that, over time, will make a difference. If you are a sponsor or counselor working with new clients in recovery, it is critical to emphasize the importance of such action steps. Let the people you work with know that even if things don't seem to be sinking in at the rational brain level at first, that's fine—in fact, it's normal in a brain that is recovering from the aftereffects of addiction and/or trauma. By taking the actions, they are taking steps to help themselves. Literally.

Reaching out to others. For newcomers, especially those who have been used to isolating, reaching out to others may seem as scary as walking down a set of train tracks in the pitch black of night with no one around to guide you. Once again, if you are working with newcomers, emphasize the importance of small steps. Going around and shaking people's hands at meetings, even if they aren't making meaningful connections, is an action step. Joining other people from the fellowship for coffee after a meeting, even if they just hang around and listen at first, is still an action step. Taking the action lays the groundwork for meaningful connections with others to eventually take place.

Prayer and other spiritual exercises. If a person is open to the spiritual aspects of a recovery program, there are ample opportunities for action. One of the reasons so many religious traditions incorporate ritual is that, for many, it can help in connecting with a Higher Power. It is no coincidence that rituals involve action.

Prayers can happen in a variety of forms, and most of those forms involve some type of action process. Whether they are getting down on their knees to say prayers in the morning or evening, driving in your car and shouting out at God, or sitting through a religious service, the body is, on some level, taking action. Even if there are no experiences of spiritual connection, taking action can serve as powerful coping mechanisms to get through difficult moments, or, when performed over time, can serve a function in helping them to develop new, more positive habits.

Consider the case of Gary, a working-class man who entered twelve-step recovery in his mid-forties. His sponsor suggested that he start praying to ask the God of his understanding to keep him sober, but Gary was resistant to this. Then, his sponsor asked Gary if he'd be willing to get on his knees every morning and say "God, help me to stay sober today," and to get on his knees every night and say, "God, thank you for keeping me sober today." These tasks were not as a spiritual exercise *per se*, but a "trick" he could try to help him stay sober, because so many people had done it before. Gary felt he had nothing to lose, and the first week or so, he reported that the words meant nothing. However, he stuck with it as a means of ritual and suggestion. Midway through the second week, he came to mean it, and at the end of the month, he surprised even himself when he realized he was still sober. What initially started as a "fake it 'til you make it" action process eventually helped Gary develop a spirituality, and he is ten years sober today.

Various twelve-step fellowships and other recovery publishers have spawned a cottage industry of daily meditation books, also excellent mechanisms to help a person take action-oriented steps along a spiritual path. I have a very personal connection to this ritual. When I first came into recovery, I had no problem believing in God, but I did have a problem disciplining myself with morning prayer. Janet, my sponsor, suggested that I place one of my daily meditation books on the toilet seat so that when I woke up in the morning, I had to pick up the book in order to lift the toilet seat! Thus, I would have it in my hands and it would remind me to start my day on a spiritual note, reading the meditation and saying a little prayer. By the end of thirty days of my toilet meditations, I formed a new habit, and now I cannot even dream of starting my day without at least a little prayer and meditation reading. Although I no longer keep the meditation book on the toilet seat, I do still keep it in my bathroom!

Recovery fellowships pass along many spiritual techniques that incorporate excellent action components. Another favorite of mine is the "God box." With the God-box technique, recovering people simply get an old shoebox, jar, or other container and put it in a special place, designating it as their "God box." Whenever a problem or issue cannot stop swirling around in their heads, they get out a piece of paper and write down what's bothering them. They fold the paper as much as they can (I like to keep folding the paper over until I can't fold it any more—it helps to work out the frustration), and then place it in the "God box." For many, the act of writing it down and "getting it out" is a key part of the healing; again, an action-oriented healing step. If, later in the day, the person, place, or situation starts swirling around again, they remind themselves, "I put it in the God box; it's out of my hands now," and bring up the visual of putting the paper in the box. When I was in early recovery, I thought this technique was a bit juvenile, but eventually I tried it and found that it worked like a charm! They can use whatever spiritual principles they like as a variation to this exercise (i.e., call it a "universe capsule," for instance instead of the term *God*).

Once the box gets full, they choose action-based activities to carry on the ritual. Some people like to clean out their God boxes every time they fill up and read through the slips of paper. They'll likely be surprised how the things that they stressed over six months ago have long resolved. At that point, some people like to take those slips of paper out of the God box and keep them in a separate thank-you box. I have even known some people who have taken great comfort in burning them (outside, of course), with the smoke rising up to the sky representing a thanksgiving. The options are endless, as long as they are meaningful to the person carrying out the ritual.

Writing. Whether it's jotting down a simple statement and placing it in a God box or spilling out their soul into an entire novel, writing provides a means of emotional release for many people in recovery. In the spirit of action-oriented intervention, I often tell my clients that the quality of what they write is not so important; what *is* important is that they take the action step of writing (which involves using the body) to get stuff out. That stuff can include obsessions, emotional angst, resentments, past memories, or simply a list of stressors that may just need to come out visibly on paper. When clients are resistant to journaling, I often tell them that I'm not going to grade it like an English paper, and if they want, they don't even have to keep what they write. In fact, I tell clients that after they write a journal entry, they have every right to rip it up (and sometimes this is therapeutic in a body-based sense…it can continue the process of working out the stress, especially if ripping up symbolizes "I don't want this anymore").

A technique we often use in trauma counseling (from the Gestalt tradition) is something called the *unsent letter*, and I am aware of many sponsors who assign some variation of this technique to twelve-step sponsees. In this process, a person writes, in letter form, everything that he would like to say to the person who offended him or traumatized him. I encourage my clients to get it all out—don't censor language or judge emotional content, just let 'er rip! Together, after they've released the emotions through the physical process of writing, we devise a method for best releasing the unsent letter. Some people choose to rip them up and leave them in the therapist's trash bin (again, symbolizing letting go and leaving it behind), whereas others may choose to burn the letter, noticing the rising smoke as a symbolic releasing of the pain in the letter to God/Higher Power. I know of others who have chosen to leave unsent letters at a cemetery, if the letter is to someone who has passed away. The options here are endless; the common denominator is that the physical processes involved with these activities powerfully activate the brain to help with the overall sense of release.

Another journal-based exercise that can be helpful is the *gratitude list*. A piece of folk knowledge in traditional recovery is that the best way out of self-pity is to foster an inner sense of gratitude. Although this may be a hard sell on people new to recovery who have had a difficult life due to trauma or other circumstances, if presented lovingly by a trusted sponsor, this technique can be quite effective. With the gratitude list, a person writes down at least ten things that he or she is grateful for at any given time. I often need to encourage my clients to get as specific as "I have a place to live right now," or "I have food to eat." Other popular entries include, "I still have my children in my life," or, "I have been able to stay sober this long." The action-oriented process of writing out the positives is therapeutic, and actually seeing the entries on paper can help a person to refocus on the positives in his life in a way that just thinking about them cannot.

For the same reasons that writing out a gratitude list can be helpful instead of just thinking about it, so too can writing out step work facilitate the process of mental retention. Different sponsors have various approaches to guiding sponsees through the twelve steps, and many choose to have sponsees write out inventories (as in step four) or make lists (as in step eight). Some fellowships, like Narcotics Anonymous, use workbook sheets to help members work each step in depth, and incorporate writing as a main mechanism for the step work. Although writing out the steps is not for everyone (this is up to the sponsor to assess on a person-by-person basis), the action that writing requires can be a beneficial part of the process, especially if it helps the individual to take further, healthier action as he works the step.

Repetition or "ritual" strategies. A few other folkways of recovery are worth sharing because they incorporate such a strong, body-based component. Anything in the spirit of ritual or repetition that can help a person to cope with or get through a moment of craving or triggers is worth sharing. We discussed the importance of using the phone earlier in the chapter. An issue that often comes up with newcomers is, "What if I can't reach someone, especially my sponsor, on the phone?" The simple answer to this legitimate question is that they need to keep calling. Even if they dial ten numbers collected at meetings and no one is there, they keep pressing ahead with the action, picking up the phone and dialing the number. The hope is that they will eventually reach somebody, but even if they don't, taking five to ten minutes to get busy with their body in the simple, healthy action of dialing may be just enough time for the craving or trigger to pass. Many people find similar relief in doing household tasks, especially scrubbing and cleaning, as a coping skill. This action makes perfect sense because it uses the body, not the mind. As a friend of mine shared once, "During my first year of sobriety, I had the cleanest toilet bowl in town...I must have scrubbed it twice a day as a coping thing!"

Gifts of coins, chips, and key chains in many fellowships mark milestones in recovery. Many people proudly carry around their thirty-day chip or nine-year coin (whatever the case may be for the person) as a form of security, a physical reminder of all they have accomplished. These physical tokens often help for coping. For instance, during a rough day, a person may pull her two-year coin out of her purse and just hold it in her hand for a few minutes; the physical sensation of the coin can allow for more effective coping because she is bringing in a body process. A humorous, but actually helpful saying that circulates in meetings when someone receives a coin or a chip is, "Now, if you ever think about drinking, put that coin on your tongue…when it dissolves, then you can have a drink." This strategy has worked for many people I know, and from a trauma-sensitive, neurological perspective, it makes sense because there is such power in the physical, more so than the cognitive, reminder.

Body 101: Powerful Coping Strategies

When I do trainings on trauma-sensitive addiction treatment, I bet I use the phrase *coping skills* a hundred times because the phrase is *that* important. The reality of recovery, especially for someone with trauma concerns, is that more unpleasant emotions, thoughts, and issues will surface the longer the alcohol or drugs have been out of the system. This idea makes total sense to anyone who has ever gone through recovery or has watched people go through the process… if you take away a person's numbing agent, he is going to start *feeling* and *experiencing* with full force, and having healthy coping skills to deal with that process is essential. Although many of the twelve-step ideas discussed in the previous section can serve as positive coping skills to help a recovering person stay stable through his adjustments, more help is often needed for coping. Coping skills that use the body and as many senses as possible are usually the most successful. Let's take a look at some popular, easy-to-learn strategies:

Breath work. Breathing is such a simple coping skill that we often miss it. Of course, we all need breath for life, yet so many of us don't take the time that we need to breathe well. For those living with the aftereffects of trauma, it can seem like they are moving through life in a state of holding their breath. Spending just a few minutes a day on some mindful, concentrated breathing can help the body and the mind more effectively cooperate with each other.

Here is a simple way to start breath work. As a start, pay attention to your normal breathing for a minute. If your mind starts to drift, that's okay, just bring the focus back to your breath. To help guide them, some people need to talk to themselves while doing the breaths (e.g., "In, 1-2-3" on the inhales, "Out, 1-2-3" on the exhales). A whole minute can be a challenge to start with—not to worry, start slowly and be gentle on yourself. If you can eventually get the breath concentration up to three minutes, you will start to notice some great benefits, and you will find that the breathing skill will be there for you to help you calm yourself when you need it most. Also, don't feel pressured to close your eyes; the breaths work just as well whether your eyes are closed or open. If you are a sponsor or counselor teaching a newcomer some basic breathing, make sure that you impart this: closing the eyes can set off a claustrophobic reaction in many traumatized people.

Once you can do the normal breath focus for at least a minute, consider experimenting with some of these other breaths and seeing if you (or those you work with) find them helpful:

- **Diaphragmatic breathing:** Otherwise known as belly breathing—simply breathe in through your nose and out through your mouth, focusing only on the rise and fall of the belly (not the whole rib cage). Expand your belly as far as it will go as you inhale inward. If it will help you, put your hand on your belly to concentrate on this "rise and fall" motion. Strive for an even inhale and exhale.

- **Complete breathing:** In this strategy, begin with the belly breath. When the stomach expands as far as it will go, take another inhale to suck in more air and concentrate on the airflow coming up into the ribs, and then the chest (you will be doing a three-part breath here). Instead of the double inhale, many people prefer spacing out half of their inhale on the belly and the other half on the chest. I often tell clients to think about themselves expanding their chests like Superman! The goal should be an even amount of airflow in and out.

- **Ujjayi breathing:** Otherwise known as "ocean breathing" or "Darth Vader breathing." This breath, which is highly effective as an affect regulator during moments of high stress/intensity is essentially a noisy in-through-the-nose, out-through-the-nose technique. The mouth should stay closed during this breath, although it should also feel as if you are sucking through a straw (this helps with stimulating nerves that help with relaxation responses). If possible, focus on contracting the muscles in the back of the throat to make the sound louder. Strive for an even inhale and exhale. Don't be afraid to get loud!

These breaths are merely a sample; there are hundreds of variations that you and those you work with can attempt. Trial and error is the key. Find which breath or combination of breaths will work the best for you and those you work with, but keep in mind a few precautions. First, start slowly. Although breathing may seem like common sense, many traumatic responses involve halted breath, and very often, trauma survivors continue living their lives breathing shallowly. Thus, stopping to pay conscious awareness to taking deep, deliberate breaths can be a new and scary experience. Don't overwhelm yourself, and be mindful that those you work with may be apprehensive at first. Taking only a couple breaths at first and focusing on an even inhale-to-exhale ratio will usually prevent any uncomfortable lightheadedness. Another precaution is that you do not have to close your eyes for breath work to be effective. So often, we think of *close your eyes and breathe* when trying to teach others the benefits of breathing, but the darkness of closed eyes can produce a claustrophobic, traumatic response in some. A sudden sense of vulnerability can take a person off guard, and this may happen when a person gets more relaxed than normal in the dark.

Although recovering individuals and sponsors can experiment with breath work on their own, please know your limits. If the breath work is causing more distress than relief, stop, and move on to another skill, or seek guidance from a professional if you are really committed to developing your breathing skills. Consider checking out the following web resources for more ideas on breath work, including a multitude of variations.

For Further Developing Breathing Skills

Dr. Andrew Weil's Homepage (Your Trusted Health Advisor)
http://www.drweil.com/drw/u/ART00521/three-breathing-exercises.html

A-B-C of Yoga
http://www.abc-of-yoga.com/pranayama/

Weintraub, A. (2012). *Yoga skills for therapists: Effective practices for mood management.* New York: W.W. Norton & Co.

Muscle relaxation. Just as breath is an inherent resource that we all have the potential to access, so too are our muscle groups. In this section, we learn how the simple act of tensing up muscle groups, relaxing them, and noticing the sensation can produce a powerful relaxation response. "Letting go" is a concept that twelve-step and other approaches to recovery discuss quite a bit. One of the classic twelve-step slogans is "Let go and let God," and many of the steps (especially four /five and eight/nine) intend for those who work them to let go of the past. Sometimes, letting go is a tough concept for alcoholics and addicts; in fact, one of the joke slogans you hear in twelve-step recovery rooms sometimes is "You know when an alcoholic has finally let go of something because it has claw marks all over it." From my experience, you can talk to a person until you are blue in the face about the benefits of letting go and how good it can feel, or you can use the body to demonstrate it. Using muscle clenching and releasing exercises offers an ideal solution. Try this powerful exercise:

"Clench & Release" for Letting Go

1) Start with your hands if this is comfortable for you. Clench your fists together as tightly as possible. Feel the nails start to dig into your skin. Notice the tension. As you do this, bring to mind a stressor or a person that is causing you distress.

2) Hold the clench as long as you can, at least five to ten seconds.

3) When you feel like you no longer want to hold on, slowly let go of the fist. Feel each finger unlock and spread out. Notice the sensation of letting go move all the way up your arm. Notice how that feels for you.

4) Take a couple of breaths of your choice (diaphragmatic works well) as you notice the feelings of release.

5) Repeat as many times as necessary until you are at your desired level of relaxation about the stressor.

OPTIONAL: You can also choose to take a deep breath in with the fist clench and hold it as you clench your fists; release the breath as you release the fists.

The great part of clench and release is that you can do it with whatever muscle group you want. For instance, I very often clench and release my feet, especially when I'm in public settings where it wouldn't be acceptable to start making fists. In fact, one of the classic progressive muscle relaxation exercises that helps people fall asleep is to clench and release one muscle group at a time (e.g., start with left fist, then left arm, left shoulder, chest, right shoulder, etc.). Hopefully, by cycling through the muscle groups and noticing the relaxation of the release, enough relaxation will induce sleep.

Many of the same precautions with muscle relaxation are similar to breath work. Recovering individuals and sponsors can experiment with some muscle relaxation on their own. It is important, however, to know your limits. Seek guidance from a professional, or consider moving on to another strategy if the muscle exercises are causing distress. These exercises are not for people with serious illness that affects muscular and orthopedic functioning unless they consult a medical professional.

Pressure points. You may associate the idea of pressure points with Eastern practices like acupuncture. The reality is that you can use knowledge that comes from such healing arts to get the blood flowing to the parts of your body where it needs to be in order to help you relax, calm, and stabilize yourself. Although my explanation of how pressure points work may be overly simplistic, this presentation is what makes the most sense to me and to many of my clients. Take a look at the photos below with explanations of how to use each pressure point. To begin, hold each pressure point for about two minutes as you breathe (again, breath of your choice, although my general guidance is to keep it simple). I find it best if you can focus on your breath as you hold the pressure point—it will enhance the relaxation response. Like with many of these skills, trial and error is key; not all of these pressure points will work for you equally well. Find the one or two that may work the best for you.

Karate Chop Point—This point assists with relaxation, and it is very handy to use if you are in a stressful setting or feeling anxious at a meeting. You can use this pressure point and go relatively unnoticed. Try alternating left and right hands (you can do one minute each to start).

Inner Gate—Use this point just below the base of your wrist, as it is an excellent point for the relief of tension and anxiety. Try alternating left and right hands (you can do one minute each to start).

Sea of Tranquility Point—This point is located at the base of the breastbone, over the heart, and is a very good pressure point for the relief of anxiety and panic.

Letting Go Points—Many like these points because you are essentially giving yourself a hug as you apply the pressure, which can add another soothing element. As the name of the points suggest, these are excellent to use when you need to release or let go of a particular stress or tension.

Gates of Consciousness Points—Think of applying pressure from your thumbs to the base of the skull. These points are very good for the release of tension, panic, and anxiety, and they also have some effect in the relief of stress headaches, irritability, or hypertension.

Clear Mind Point (Variation 1)—Take a look at this photo. It probably looks like something that you do anyway during stress. Next time, try holding it out and breathing with it for the full two minutes, and you may be surprised how it may help you soothe or regulate intense emotions.

Clear Mind Point (Variation 2)—Use this pressure point right in the center of your forehead if you are looking for an increased sense of concentration. This place right in the center of your brain is associated with mindful awareness.

Resources on Pressure Points and Other "Tapping" Strategies

Parnell, L. (2008). *Tapping in: A step-by-step guide to activating your healing resources through bilateral stimulation.* Boulder, CO: Sounds True Books.

Petrone, E. (2003). *The miracle ball method: Relieve your pain, reshape your body, and reduce your stress.* New York: Workman Publishing Company.

Waldeck, F. (2011). *Jin shin jyutsu: Guide to quick aid and healing from A–Z through the laying on of hands.* Munich: Creative-Story.

Mindfulness. There has been a great deal of buzz in mental health treatment circles in recent years about the concept of mindfulness, an ancient Buddhist practice. A simple definition of *mindfulness* comes from Buddhist teacher John Kabat-Zinn (1994): "Mindfulness means paying attention in a particular way: on purpose, in the presence of the moment, and non-judgmentally"

(p. 4). The practice of mindfulness may sound like common sense, but it can be a difficult, new intervention for trauma survivors fixated on the past or addicted people obsessed about the future. However, it surprises people who are willing to give it a try how much the practice of mindfulness helps them to relax and ultimately achieve greater focus.

One of the simplest ways to begin practicing mindfulness is to pick an object in a room that captures your attention—it can be anything, from a picture of a daisy on the wall to the fan that is blowing in the corner. To start, try for a minute to stay focused only on that object. What does it look like? What colors do you notice? What textures are you picking up on? Is there a sound, smell, taste, or any other type of sensation that goes along with the object you selected? If so, notice those. Use all of your senses in the process. Be gentle on yourself. If you can start with only a minute, that is wonderful. As you become more comfortable with practicing mindfulness, you may find that you are able to engage in this meditative practice longer.

I often suggest mindfulness strategies for clients of mine who have problems with staying focused during meetings. For instance, one of my clients carries a marble around in her pocket at all times. If she notices herself getting anxious or feels triggered at a meeting, she pulls the marble out of her pocket. She notices its dominant blue color and other hues within the glass. As she rubs the marble between her fingers, she feels the coolness of the glass and the smoothness of the texture. Then, she often experiments with rolling the marble between the palms of both of her hands, just noticing, nonjudgmentally. Typically, after about two to three minutes of this practice, she feels much more relaxed and, ultimately, is better able to focus at her twelve-step meeting. A similar process works with twelve-step meeting coins or chips; many twelve-step group members already carry these symbols around in their pockets. Another simple meeting strategy I suggest is to rub your hands on your jeans or pants, just noticing the texture of the material and the heat that your hands generate. If you draw your attention to this process mindfully, your focus on the anxiety is likely to diminish.

It is important for members of twelve-step groups who are sponsors or members who have been around a while to recognize that trauma survivors may need to engage in simple practices like the ones described here in order to stay present at meetings. Furthermore, it may also be helpful for newer members who experience high levels of anxiety at meetings to step out of the main meeting room for a few minutes and practice mindful breathing. This suggestion does not give newcomers an excuse to miss the whole meeting and stand outside smoking cigarettes (which often happens), but it ought to raise our collective awareness in twelve-step meetings that sometimes people need to step out for a while in order to stabilize, return, and then actually get something out of the meeting.

Resources on Mindfulness

Gunaratana, B. (2011). *Mindfulness in plain English: 20th anniversary edition.* Somerville, MA: Wisdom Press.

Hahn, T.N. (1999). *The miracle of mindfulness: An introduction to the practice of meditation.* Boston: The Beacon Press.

Siegel, R. (2009). *The mindfulness solution: Everyday practices for everyday problems.* New York: The Guilford Press.

Music. Famed writer Maya Angelou (1974) once wrote, "Music was my refuge. I could crawl into the space between the notes and curl my back to loneliness." This quote is just one of many that the famous (and infamous) throughout the ages have expressed about the important role music has played in helping them cope. Even Friedrich Nietzsche said, "Without music, life would be a mistake." The benefits of music on brain development are well documented in research literature (Levintin, 2006), and for many individuals in recovery, songs carry great significance. Music, which is an excellent body-based intervention because it incorporates the sense of sound and reaches parts of the brain that we cannot access simply by talking or thinking, can be applied in a variety of ways to enhance relaxation and promote empowerment in addicted survivors of trauma.

In this age of MP3 players and CD burning, the playlist or mix CD have become very popular. We can take these capacities and build them into a recovery tool. I often encourage my clients to put together a playlist or mix CD of songs that they find significant to recovery—music that either helps them relax or helps them to feel inspired. Sometimes, I encourage them to make two playlists: one relaxing, to help with issues like sleep deprivation, and one that's empowering, to help when they are facing a difficult life challenge.

People can benefit from music as part of their recovery whether they are using a simple playlist model or whether they choose to meditate on a specific piece of music when faced with a difficult situation. For instance, a person may need to listen to one of her relaxing songs in the car before she feels stable enough to walk into a meeting. When I have encountered some difficult pitfalls in recovery when it comes to standing up for myself, I often have to meditate on one of my empowering songs to get that extra emotional lift. Some people with musical talents have really used their talents in a special way to help with their recovery processes. Many recovery music websites feature the work of artists in recovery who have used songwriting and creativity to help them work through issues. Although I have been a musician all my life, I did not start writing songs until I got sober, and I found songwriting to be an outstanding outlet for catharsis.

Drum circles have also grown in popularity in recent years. Drumming is an ancient art practiced by many indigenous cultures, both to promote community and to help people "move energy" through sound and action. Drumming is an excellent, body-based intervention to use as both a coping skill and later as a reprocessing strategy. Like with dancing, physical exercise, and other formal psychotherapies, such as EMDR, drumming incorporates bilateral stimulation, the brain's inherent mechanism for promoting processing and restoring equilibrium. The nice thing about drumming is that a person can join a drum circle or perhaps attend a workshop on drumming (yoga studios and performing arts centers often host such workshops), or a person can simply enhance sound and body release by creating his own percussion at home. Tabletops are excellent for improvisation, and a person can even engage in foot stomping or toe tapping as a means of percussive, energy release.

Imagery. The technique of imagery, sometimes called *guided imagery,* has many applications. Most professional therapists use some form of guided imagery in their work with clients, and others focus on guided imagery as their special modality in the treatment of trauma. Indeed, imagery is powerful, utilizing the potential of the human imagination for therapeutic benefit. Counselors often use safe or calm-place imageries to allow their clients to tap into positive feelings by using a series of pictures or imagined experiences. Imagery is also beneficial for deeper trauma work as well as being a mechanism through which the person can visualize the memory of the trauma, thus allowing him to encounter unresolved images, thoughts, experiences, or feelings, and hopefully reprocess them to some point of resolution.

I recommend that most people begin guided imagery work under the guidance of a professional, especially if the person has significant unresolved trauma. Although imagery may sound as simple as "picture yourself in your happy place," sometimes these happy or safe places can bring up some negative emotions as well, and it helps to have that extra guidance of someone clinically trained. People in recovery, when properly instructed in these methods, can apply them when emotional distress comes up as part of twelve-step meetings or in the completion of step work. Check out the inset called Resources on Guided Imagery if you are interested in reading more about guided imagery as a positive recovery resource.

Resources on Guided Imagery

Lusk, J. T. (Ed.) (1992). *30 scripts for relaxation and healing imagery.* Duluth, MN: Whole Person Associates.

Naparstek, B. R. (1994). *Staying well with guided imagery.* New York: Warner Books/Grand Central Publishing.

Naparstek, B. R. (2004). *Invisible heroes: Survivors of trauma and how they heal.* New York: Bantam Books.

Toolkit Strategy: Experiential Learning

In order to be truly effective in relaying these skills to your clients and those you work with in recovery, it is important that you experience them for yourself. As a way of building your own trauma toolkit for working with others, complete at least three of the activities described in this chapter. If you really want to expand your skill set, go ahead and give them all a try!

CHAPTER 8

It's the Relationship That Heals

When I required addiction treatment ten years ago, I didn't go to one of those fancy treatment centers that I saw advertised on the Internet, nor did I even seek out a twelve-step group in my own community...I moved to Bosnia. As a twenty-one-year-old American expatriate vagabond seeking some kind of solution for the emptiness that I felt inside, I thought that working in the third world for a few years would help me "find myself." Yes, my move was a geographical cure at the time, but it was in the hills of Bosnia-Hercegovina that I was led to an orange humanitarian aid trailer that would become my treatment center. In it, I learned one of the most valuable lessons about healing addiction in a trauma-sensitive manner: it's the relationship that heals. My mentor/sponsor, Janet, who I introduced you to in chapter 6, had access to a large, garishly orange trailer that had once served as a priest's makeshift office. At the time we met, it stored his books, but there was a desk and a few chairs inside as well. It was in this trailer that I first revealed to Janet, initially just a social worker who I met during my service in Bosnia, that I believed I had a problem with chemicals. It was in this trailer that she explained to me the disease of addiction and the implications for treating it, and it was in this trailer that we met on an almost biweekly basis, engaging in the healing conversations that would become the basis of my own recovery. It was in this trailer that she first delivered the line that would be pivotal in my recovery, later guiding the work I do with others: "Jamie, after everything you've been through, no wonder you became an alcoholic [validation]…but what are you going to do about it now [challenge to action]?"

This was my "treatment center"—For a full color photo, go to www.TraumaTwelve.com/orangetrailer
Photo by Janet L.

There is a misconception that to begin healing from the wounds of addiction and trauma, a person needs sophisticated treatment. While structured, trauma-informed treatment centers have helped countless addicted individuals get well, there is no inherent magic in the treatment centers that promotes healing. However, it is what these centers and programs have the potential to promote—forging of healthy, recovery-oriented relationships—that we must consider as the most powerful healing mechanisms of action. This chapter imparts critical knowledge about the importance of the relationship in the healing process, especially if you are promoting trauma-sensitive addiction recovery. This chapter also presents suggestions for promoting the highest levels of empathy and being effective in forging therapeutic relationships. What you *are* and how you deal with a person is typically more significant than anything you can say: this guiding principle is at the heart of the chapter, and it is a principle that I hope you can embrace regardless of your role or chosen therapeutic paradigm.

"The Gift" of a Healing Relationship

I get very concerned when I hear professionals giving Carl Rogers a bad rap; when I was in graduate school, I was especially shocked. Although my professors requisitely covered client-centered therapy as we went through the many theories of counseling, they described Rogers as too "nondirective." His three central skills—unconditional positive regard, empathy, and congruence—although labeled "important," seemed to be downplayed next to the cognitive-behavioral interventions that we were learning. A message that I received in my early training was that if we really wanted to see changes in our patients, we needed to get in there and *do* something. When a friend of mine interviewed for her first job after graduate school, the program director asked her which school of therapy best described her. Being an eclectic who believed in both direct intervention and the importance of forging a therapeutic alliance, she replied, "I guess I would consider myself a firm Carl Rogers. Simply mentioning Rogers sunk her. The interviewer rolled his eyes and retorted, "Well, we're really very cognitive-behavioral around here."

In this age of evidence-based treatment, the critical importance of the therapeutic relationship is on the back burner. Let's consider for a moment what evidenced-based practice really means, as defined by the American Psychological Association (2006): the best available research with clinical expertise in the context of patient characteristics, culture, and preferences. Thus, if we operate on straight intervention, no matter how much research support it has, we are being ignorant providers if we ignore what the client brings to the table. Let's explore further.

Research supports those of us who espouse that the quality of a therapeutic relationship rests at the heart of what we do as helpers. Honoring the therapeutic relationship and taking the necessary steps to building a quality working alliance between you and your client are absolutely essential when using or executing any healing intervention for addiction. Respecting the therapeutic relationship is one simple factor that enhances our work with clients (Marich, 2011).

While working on my PhD, I attended a workshop led by a senior addiction counselor who recommended that I read *The Gift of Therapy* by Irving Yalom (2001).

"Yalom?" I questioned, "Isn't he the guy who wrote the thousand-page text on group therapy?"

"Yes," answered my colleague, "But The Gift of Therapy is different." It's written by a much older Yalom, who has learned from his mistakes, declaring that despite all of his years writing about techniques, it really is the relationship that matters most.

The book absolutely changed my life and my approach to clinical work.

Yalom contends that therapy should not be theory driven, but relationship driven. Paying attention to existential issues can deeply influence the nature of the therapeutic relationship and the therapy itself. In Yalom's view, a therapist has no place forcing solutions, a piece of guidance I first heard while attending meetings of Al-Anon family groups. When I began applying many of Yalom's principles to my own clinical work (principles he clearly traces back to Carl Rogers), I noticed that my own heightened effectiveness in working with clients, and my client outcomes reflected the improvement.

A major point that Yalom highlighted, serving as a salient learning point for counselors and sponsors alike, is that my view of a therapy session as a professional may be drastically different from a client's view. In other words, we may think that we are relaying such directive wisdom to our clients or sponsees, but it may be totally going over their heads. In contrast, a simple smile that we give to the person we're working with as they share something with us may strike us as insignificant, but it might be powerfully healing to the client. Yalom expounds upon this phenomenon in another work, *Every Day Gets a Little Closer: A Twice-Told Therapy* (Yalom & Elkin, 1974). This book chronicled a year Yalom spent doing therapy with one particular client, Ginny Elkin. After each session, Yalom would write his reflections of the session down, and then Ginny would do the same. Yalom's reflections focused on technique and all of the "brilliant" things he said and did in the session. For the client, the impact of the session was all in the relationship (Marich, 2011).

Although these relational ideas of Yalom's may be too flowery and passive, research supports them. Let's take a look at some of these works and their implications. In their collected volume, *The Heart and Soul of Change: What Works in Psychotherapy*, Duncan, Miller, Wampold, & Hubbard (2009) concluded that the collaborative, therapeutic alliance between client and clinician is a primary factor in determining successful therapy outcomes and is more important than the specific execution of therapeutic protocols. They also stressed that obtaining continuous client feedback throughout the therapeutic process is a critical component in enhancing client care. In other words, check in with the client either quantitatively or qualitatively to make sure that what you are working on and how you are approaching the recovery plan is really working for them. This idea runs counter to some of the logic promoted in traditional recovery circles: If addicted people messed up their lives so badly, shouldn't they just sit back and take suggestions? Although taking new suggestions is an important part of lifestyle change, we must not ignore the fact that the people we work with really are the best experts on the subject of their life.

The collective body of research, as presented in *The Heart and Soul of Change*, shows that little difference exists among the specific factors (e.g., specific techniques or interventions) of bona fide, researched therapies intended to be therapeutic. Thus, assignment to a twelve-step facilitation group versus a cognitive-behavioral therapy group does not automatically determine a person's success in treatment. Rather, a series of four *common factors*, working in concert, contribute to a person's overall change. These common factors are the clients and their extra-therapeutic factors (e.g., what they bring to the table in therapy and situations out of the control of the clinician), models and techniques that work to engage and inspire the client, the therapeutic relationship/alliance, and therapist factors. As the editors of *The Heart and Soul of Change* describe:

> "We conclude that what happens (when a client is confronting negative schema, addressing family boundaries, or interpreting transference) is less important than the degree to which any particular activity is consistent with the

therapist's beliefs and values (allegiances) while concurrently fostering the client's hope (expectations). Allegiance and expectancy are two sides of the same coin: the faith of both the therapist and the client in the restorative power and credibility of the therapy's rationale and related rituals. Though rarely viewed this way, models and techniques work best when they engage and inspire the participants" (p. 37).

Interestingly, a New York psychiatrist named Saul Rosenzweig first proposed the common factors in 1936, predating the work of Rogers and Yalom. Rosenzweig, even in his era, grew concerned with schools of therapy that zealously believed their approach was the *right way*, battles amongst philosophical approaches that continue to this day. Rosenzweig essentially contended that by focusing on what is similar amongst approaches as we deliver services, we will be in the position to influence the most change. This idea is inherently trauma-sensitive.

Norcross made similar conclusions in *Psychotherapy Relationships That Work: Therapist Contributions and Responsiveness to Patients* (2002). Using a collection of empirical research studies, Norcross proved that the therapy relationship, together with discrete method, influences treatment outcomes. Norcross challenged therapists and helpers to hone these relational elements, noting that it is their responsibility to tailor these skills to the needs of individual patients. Thus, the relationship should drive the theory, not the other way around (Marich, 2011).

We should not just throw theory and technique out the window—it is clearly important. However, if we are adhering to technical elements or holding true to our chosen philosophy or paradigm out of principle at the expense of the relationship, then there is a problem. Consider this metaphor: If we put theory or philosophy in the driver's seat (e.g., twelve-step principles, cognitive-behavioral therapy) and shove the relationship all the way back into the trunk of the car, the therapy isn't going to go anywhere. The therapeutic relationship needs to take the front seat. Carrying the metaphor one step further, let the client steer the course of the treatment and allow yourself as the counselor or helper to serve as the trusted front-seat navigator. At times, the client may need a rest, and you will need to take the wheel for a while. The technique is like a navigating passenger in the backseat with a map or GPS system. It can give you good direction, especially when you're lost, but ultimately, the technique or philosophy should never be the entity actually doing the driving. Keep this in mind as well: sometimes maps are hard to read and don't take into account the creative elements of a drive (e.g., point A to point B may look quicker, but if you've actually driven it before, you know there may be a better way to go). The driving-navigation metaphor becomes especially relevant in considering how to most effectively treat an addicted client with unresolved trauma. The literature in general traumatic stress studies indicates that the therapeutic alliance is an important mechanism in facilitating meaningful change for clients with complex PTSD, the most salient predictor of outcome success in treatment of such clients (Fosha, 2000; Fosha & Slowiaczek, 1997; Pearlman & Courtois, 2005).

Enhancing Empathy: The Key to a Strong Therapeutic Alliance

Forging a strong therapeutic alliance does not mean that you have to become your client's best friend. In fact, allowing that to happen can actually be counter-therapeutic. Rather, my view of a solid working alliance is that the person you are working with trusts you, can relate to you, believes that you relate to her, and trusts that the work you are doing together is helping her get well. In our discussion of best practices for working with addicted survivors of trauma in chapter 6, we concluded that being the best version of yourself is usually the best approach to take in working with addicted survivors of trauma; genuineness is key with this population. To really take the therapeutic alliance to a healing level, empathy must also be present.

Technical definitions abound in the psychotherapeutic professions to describe empathy. For the purposes of establishing a working base, let us consider the American Psychological Association's (VandenBos, 2007; p.327) dictionary definition of empathy:

> understanding a person from his or her own frame of reference rather than
> one's own, so that one vicariously experiences the person's feelings, perceptions,
> and thoughts; in psychotherapy, therapist empathy for the client can be a path
> to comprehension of the client's cognitions, affects, and behaviors.

Most would agree that empathy, which calls for us to step into another's shoes and see life from his perspective, is a stronger degree of engagement with another than sympathy, which usually implies simply identifying with the feelings of an another.

Authors Bruce Perry, MD, PhD, and journalist Maia Szalavitz, make this useful distinction between empathy and sympathy:

> The essence of empathy is the ability to stand in another's shoes, to feel
> what it's like there and care about making it better if it hurts….When you
> empathize with someone, you try to see and feel the world from his or her per-
> spective. Your primary feelings are more related to the other person's situation
> than your own. But when you sympathize, while you understand what others are
> going through, you don't necessarily feel it yourself right now, though you may
> be moved to help nonetheless. Pity—or feeling sorry for someone—similarly
> captures the idea of recognizing another's pain without simultaneously experi-
> encing a sense of it oneself. With empathy, however, you feel the other person's
> pain. You're feeling sorry "with" them, not just "for" them (pp. 12–13).

As a brief pause in your reading, it may be useful for you to consider these distinctions and ask yourself whether or not, as a helper, you have been more likely to display sympathy or empathy.

To truly practice empathy as therapists, which ultimately forges a clear path therapeutically as the APA definition suggests, we who work with addicted survivors of trauma must be able to proverbially step into the shoes of the people that we are treating. If we as helpers come across as experts, we run an extremely high chance of alienating this population. However, by approaching the addicted survivors of trauma that we are working with as empathetic collaborators, we will be able to more effectively foster therapeutic change. Let's consider some of the ways, as helpers, that we can build upon the empathetic abilities we may already possess.

Most would argue that a counselor without empathy is just as dangerous as a surgeon who can't keep his hand steady while making an incision. Empathy is such an important component of what defines the helping professions, yet I have too often observed that the farther removed a helper is from suffering, the more potential she exhibits to lose her empathetic abilities. I see this happen in two major ways. First, counselors and other helpers sometimes enter the professions without having experienced any major life suffering, or if they have, they have never taken active measures to *do their own healing work*, so to speak. Such helpers are usually prone to falling into the role of expert without ever developing true empathy. Second, I have also encountered professionals, and even recovery sponsors, who begin their vocations with a high degree of empathy. However, either through burnout or through moving on with their lives so much they forget what it's like to be a newcomer struggling with sobriety, their potential for empathy can diminish.

One of the first steps in building our empathy potential is to approach what we do with an open heart and mind. No matter how accomplished we may be in our fields, how many degrees we have, or how many people we have sponsored or mentored over the years, stepping out of the expert role to really learn from our clients is a critical component. By first adopting this open mind, there are a variety of steps we can take to build our empathetic potential: attending open twelve-step meetings, volunteering at a homeless shelter or with another community project that serves the underprivileged, reading first-person accounts of addiction and/or trauma recovery, watching movies about those struggling with recovery, and simply viewing our patients or sponsees as teachers when they share with us. However, a professional can engage in all of these activities, and if they do so with a closed mind and a mighty ego, these exercises may be futile.

In essence, if we find ourselves growing cold or bitter toward clients, we need to be able to find some way to step into their shoes and get a glimpse of what it is like to suffer as they are suffering. For us professionals in recovery or those of us who have dealt with major life traumas in the past, sometimes the simple act of allowing our minds to float back and tap into the memories can give us the necessary stimulus. For counselors in recovery or recovery sponsors, sharing their personal stories at twelve-step meetings or in community forums, perhaps even self-disclosing appropriately in a group or individual treatment setting, can also prove to be potent reminders.

In my view, the best counselors, sponsors, and helpers to work with recovering individuals dealing with trauma are not necessarily those in recovery themselves, but rather those who continue to work on themselves and the struggles life brings their way. Life doesn't stop when we become counselors or sponsors. Willingness to continue our own healing quests will make us better at what we do, especially if we are practicing with a trauma toolkit.

Toolkit Strategy: Self-Evaluation

Consider this list of characteristics that ten women, all of whom completed addiction treatment within a trauma-sensitive setting, identified as being reflective of their experiences with counselors (Marich, 2010): Take a look down each list. Which characteristics on the positive side do you strive to exhibit? Which do you exhibit especially well? On the negative side, which characteristic might you struggle with that you have the potential to address?

Positive experiences	Negative experiences
caring	rigid
trustworthy	scripted
intuitive	detached
natural	anxious
connected	unclear
comfortable with trauma work	uncomfortable with trauma
skilled	
accommodating	
magical	
wonderful	
commonsensical	
validating	
gentle	
nurturing	
facilitating	
smart	
consoling	
"The bomb"	

It Takes a Village: Fostering Multi-Leveled Relationships

Relationships heal. This premise guides this chapter, and indeed this book. However, in the spirit of growth and development as empathetic counselors, it is also important to realize that we, as helpers, are not solely responsible for helping a client get sober and well. Too often, professionals (and many recovery sponsors) feel so overly responsible for the success or failure of their clients/sponsees that they lose perspective on the idea that no singular factor helps a person, especially a traumatized person, obtain recovery. Although I explore this idea more fully in the next chapter, it is worth mentioning here since we have spent the chapter discussing relationships. All relationships have the potential to heal, not just the relationship between therapist and client or between sponsor and sponsee. Thus, as facilitators of a person's recovery experience, one of the most trauma-proficient steps we can take is to help a person keep his eyes open to the potentially meaningful relationships around him and discover how these relationships can aid in recovery.

The term *support system* often describes the people surrounding a person who literally support her recovery and have her best interests at heart. Interestingly, the term *support system* appears in many more contexts than just addiction recovery in our culture—those recovering from physical diseases like cancer often cite the importance of a support system, and you often hear new parents credit the importance of a support system in helping them to adjust. The logic is simple: support systems consist of people who are on your side, people who are in a position to help you who also love you enough to call you out if you are doing something destructive to your recovery. With the exception of a very few approaches to recovery that support self-sufficiency (most notably Rational Recovery), a hallmark of most recovery programs is the importance of building a solid support system. As counselors or sponsors, we are in a golden position to help people identify which people in their lives they can use as healthy supports and to help clients recognize the teachable moments with people and relationships that are all around them.

In addition to Janet, my first sponsor, one of my wisest teachers during my time in Bosnia was a four-year-old girl named Anita. She is clearly someone who came into my life at a time when I needed to learn from her noble example, and her influence on me proves that healing in relationships can come in all forms. Anita was one of the children living in Mother's Village, a foster home where I tutored young Croatian and Bosnian students in English and music. Mother's Village featured a fabulous swing set, and every day, Anita would watch the other children on the swings with curiosity. Although she wanted to partake in all the fun, Anita found herself too afraid to try. Eventually, I coaxed her into giving the swings a try with her sitting on my lap, and she soon felt brave enough to give the swings a go on her own. A few days later, Anita began to push the boundaries of her curiosity, swinging higher and higher with each attempt.

Then, what I thought was bound to be tragedy struck. While attempting to swing and then jump off in mid-air for a graceful landing below (a maneuver that she saw many of the older kids try), Anita fell. Initially she cried, and I came over to hug her and see if she was okay. I thought, "Oh no, she's finally on the swings, and now this had to happen! She's not going to want to go near them again." But the resilient Anita proved me wrong. After a minute or two of tears, she went back on the swing again, this time swinging higher than she ever had before. She even cried out joyously, "Look at me; I'm not afraid anymore...I'm not afraid anymore!"

All of this happened at a time in my own life when I was trying to sort out my past wounds and embrace my own personal recovery. My experience of working with Anita, and seeing her resilient example, helped to quell my initial fears about recovery in a way that nothing else really has. This four-year-old child, riddled with her own trauma of being born into such a chaotic sociopolitical environment, helped me to tap into my own sense of resilience. Even to this day, whenever I struggle with a fear issue, I think of Anita's smiling laughter as she played on the swing.

Relationships heal. Relationships most definitely heal, sometimes in a way that we least expect them to heal. Helping clients and those new to recovery to see the healing potential in each relationship, even if that relationship just provides an opportunity to set a boundary and thus promote personal growth, is one of most powerful tools in trauma-informed treatment.

For Further Reading

Perry, B. D., & Szalavitz, M. (2010). *Born for love: Why empathy is essential—and endangered.* New York: Harper

Yalom, I. (2001). *The gift of therapy: Reflections on being a therapist.* London, England: Piatkus.

Yalom, I., & Elkin, G. (1974). *Each day gets a little closer: A twice-told therapy.* New York: Basic Books.

Toolkit Strategy: Step into Their Shoes— Skills for Empathy Building

Think of someone that you currently work with in your role as a counselor, helping professional, or recovery sponsor/ leader. If you are not currently working with people in recovery, you can use a past case, or even bring a "celebrity" case to mind for this exercise.

Bring to mind a picture of that person. Notice what that individual looks like. Notice the identifying traits: gender, race, ethnicity, height, body type, any distinguishing physical features. Pay attention to what he or she may be wearing upon walking into your facility, or maybe into a recovery meeting. Think about what brought that person there in the first place. Is he there because he wants to be there? Is she there because someone told her she had to be there? Think about how that person literally got there. If you're in a hospital setting, did the client come by ambulance or by car? If you're in an agency or office setting, did your client drive herself there or did she take the bus? Maybe she walked or maybe someone gave her a lift. If you are so willing, take a moment and actually "step into the shoes" of the person that you brought to mind. Now take a few moments and notice. Notice what is going through your mind as you walk into this facility or into this recovery meeting for the first time. Notice how you are feeling. Notice what is happening in your body. Take a few minutes and just be with this experience.

When you are ready, step back into the role of yourself as the reader of this book, knowing that you can access this experience any time that you need to step into the shoes of another.

Find an extended audio version of this exercise on the CD companion, go to www.TraumaTwelve.com

CHAPTER 9

Best Practices for Building Recovery Capital

In reflecting back on her treatment experience after four years in recovery from heroin addiction, Cindy noted, "I see the quality of work that I did here as a client, and it's incomparable to the other treatment centers that I have seen, because of the focus on trauma." The *here* that Cindy is referring to is Amethyst, Inc., a treatment program for addicted women in Columbus, Ohio. As we examine Cindy's story in greater depth, we see how having her traumatic experiences and individual preferences respected as part of the treatment process was vital to her success.

Cindy's "taste for opiates," as she calls it, started at age fifteen when she developed a chronic kidney stone condition. Cindy's addiction progressed to polysubstance use, injecting combinations of cocaine and heroin just prior to entering treatment at Amethyst. From adolescence, Cindy acquired a variety of mental health diagnoses, including ADHD, depression, complex PTSD, bipolar disorder, obsessive-compulsive disorder, anxiety/social phobia, and borderline personality disorder. Cindy indicated that she first received the diagnosis of borderline personality disorder in her teens. The diagnosis was not surprising considering that by that age of fifteen, Cindy already experienced a plethora of abandonment-related trauma, in addition to the alienation she felt due to identifying as lesbian at a Catholic school.

Prior to entering Amethyst, a hospital-based treatment center detoxified Cindy and then sent her to treatment at a residential facility. However, after charting some clean time, Cindy's mental health issues began to emerge in full force, especially dissociative symptoms, and the residential treatment center did not know how to care for Cindy. Thus, they sent her to Amethyst so that she could receive the holistic, trauma-sensitive help that she needed. Cindy was able to stay involved with the Amethyst program for a two-year period, accessing trauma-sensitive outpatient groups and EMDR therapy to help her work through her traumatic experiences and their impact on her mental health symptoms. For Cindy, this trauma-sensitive approach was especially significant because she had problems accepting twelve-step recovery due to her struggles with religion and spirituality.

The Amethyst program also assisted Cindy in going back to school. She was able to complete an associate's degree in substance abuse counseling at a community college, and she is currently working on finishing a bachelor's degree, with the goal of going for a master's. Cindy was required to complete an internship at a drug and alcohol treatment center as part of her associate's degree. When she began her work at the traditional facility to which the school assigned her, she was horrified. Cindy shared, "Some of the women at this facility are able to stay up to six months, and the staff is doing nothing to address the trauma…and these women have layers and layers of it. Don't you think they would want to start addressing some of those layers?" After completing her internship, Cindy became even more grateful for the treatment she received at Amethyst.

Cindy's experience at Amethyst allowed her to acquire and foster *recovery capital*, a concept that we explore in this chapter. Recovery capital is the "quality and quantity of internal and external resources that one can bring to bear on the initiation and maintenance of recovery" (Granfield & Cloud, 1999; White & Kurtz, 2006, p. 9). In other words, these are the tangible and intangible resources that an individual can call upon to make recovery successful. Recovery capital can include a support group, twelve-step meetings, a sponsor, a church group, a job, hobbies, supportive family, motivation, and a place to live—essentially, whatever the person has going for him or her. Granfield and Cloud, two authors who fundamentally oppose twelve-step programming, coined this phrase in part to demonstrate that it's not necessarily the specific program or therapeutic approach that helps a person get sober; rather, how a person acquires and uses the capital is paramount.

In trauma-informed addiction treatment, helping clients to identify and to build upon their recovery capital is an essential function of initial stabilization. Before a client can proceed with the cathartic activities that are normally associated with "trauma work," having a foundation of safety and coping skills is critical, a point of repeated emphasis in this book. As we will cover in this chapter, we are in a position to help a client identify and build upon this recovery capital, thus beginning the process of lifestyle change required for meaningful, trauma-sensitive recovery.

Recovery Capital 101

To most effectively demonstrate the concept of recovery capital and its importance, I'd like you to take a minute and consider what the recovery capital is in your own life. Even if you are not in recovery, per se, take a moment and consider what you have going for you. Do you have a place to live? Food to eat? A stable income? A supportive family? A strong work ethic? A moral compass? These are just some examples. If you are willing, take a few moments and really identify everything you have that contributes to you living a functional life—this can include elements that exist in your life that perhaps you are not currently accessing to their fullest potential.

A potent principle of the positive psychology approach is not just to focus on the problems that a person identifies. It is just as important to identify what a person has done right, to bolster the positive elements of a person's life as a means of helping her address the identified problems. This approach may be a bit of a paradigm shift for some twelve-step traditionalists who hang onto slogans like, "Your best thinking got you here," or to others who approach addiction as a moral/criminal problem alone. However, this positive approach is essentially trauma-sensitive. Remember, individuals struggling with addiction and trauma are likely coming for help with an already ingrained shame-based identity. It will be a radical, new intervention for a professional or sponsor to be able to help them identify what is good, right, or healthy about their lives.

For some of our clients, identifying the good can be a challenge. Most of us have had the experience of having clients come up empty when asked to name even one positive quality about themselves. Other clients come into treatment or a recovery program so weathered by life, helping them access the basic essentials of life such as safe/sober housing, food, and transportation can prove challenging. However, as the classic Maslow hierarchy approach would suggest, helping a person access these basic needs is a critical part of trauma-informed care. As a client of mine once shared, "If I don't have a place to sleep tonight or food to eat, the last thing I want to think about is going to a [recovery] meeting." While traditionalists may argue with that logic, what my client shared is exactly what most traumatized individuals feel who present for treatment with little recovery capital.

Thus, as professional or recovery group leaders working in our community, it is imperative that we familiarize ourselves with the various resources available to the people we work with and understand how they are able to access them. I am not just talking about finding out which recovery meetings are out there and which ones are solid (see chapter 6 for more on this topic); although this task is definitely a part of helping a client build recovery capital, we can take it further. When I first started working in community-based drug and alcohol treatment, I had to attend (kicking and screaming) a two-day orientation on all the services available to residents of our county. We were literally required to get in our cars as part of the training and drive from site to site like a poker run. To this day, this experience remains one of the most valuable trainings that I participated in as a professional. It really got me to think about what is available for people. Although I can access many community-based resources today simply by using an Internet search engine, networking, or using the telephone, this initial training experience opened my eyes to how services are out there to address many needs.

Toolkit Strategy: Accessing Resources and Recovery Capital

For those of you who already excel at accessing community resources, this exercise may seem repetitive. However, you may be surprised at what else you might find out there by doing this exercise, so go ahead and give it a try!

Think about the last client or recovering person you worked with who had a major survival need, like lack of adequate housing, inability to obtain furniture, or a need to acquire legal help in applying for Social Security disability. Go on an Internet search engine or pick up the phone to call someone with whom you regularly network in your community and find out what may be available in your community and how a person can access it. Feel free to repeat this exercise as many times as necessary; always be willing to expand your knowledge base when it helps to point a person in the direction of resources.

Case management is a vital yet often overlooked function of early recovery. According to the twelve core functions of alcohol and other drug treatment, a model incorporated by many state boards to license chemical dependency counselors (not to be confused with the twelve steps), case management encompasses activities that bring services, agencies, resources, or people together within a planned framework of action toward the achievement of established goals. Case management may involve liaison activities and collateral contacts. Simply put, it involves those activities that fall outside the scope of psychotherapy yet are still indelibly vital to the healing process. Solid case management can promote enhanced therapy and treatment.

Many treatment centers have the resources at their disposal to have separate case managers working with individuals in treatment, apart from the primary counselor. Depending on resources available in the community or certain benefits allowed with state-appropriated services (e.g., Medicaid), many clients can access separate case management services in addition to accessing traditional therapy. Finding out if case management services (the names of these services can vary from state to state) are available is vital to a trauma-informed treatment plan.

Some of the most successful episodes of treatment I have witnessed in my career of working with very complicated clients have come when I as the counselor am able to work together with a separate case manager. It frees up time in counseling sessions for psychotherapeutic activities instead of activities that may fall under the realm of case management. Moreover, a solid case manager can provide a client with another outlet of caring support. I have witnessed some of the most outstanding healing relationships forge between client and case manager, a construct that I expounded upon in the previous chapter.

Toolkit Strategy: Assets and Debits

To help a client evaluate the capital he has going for him in the service of his recovery, a helpful strategy is to have him (with your help in a session if needed) evaluate what he has going for him in the service of his recovery, compared to what may be holding him back. I have included a clean copy of a worksheet that you can use for this activity in chapter 10. A filled out worksheet may look something like this: (You may recognize him as the character Justin Walker from the TV series Brothers & Sisters).

Justin's Recovery: Assets and Debits

ASSETS	DEBITS
insurance to access treatment (VA)	lots of drinking/using friends
supportive family	some co-dependent family members
brother Tommy: calls me out on behavior	mom enables me with money/excuse
place to live in good neighborhood (mom's)	mom keeps wine in house
supportive/effective twelve-step sponsor	lacks discipline about praying
access/transportation to meetings	sexual relationship with girl who still drinks
believes in God	military-related PTSD/nightmares
military experience taught discipline	no job
time to go to meetings	lying, manipulation are engrained character
loves nieces/nephews: wants to be there	traits
afraid of driving car to bad neighborhood	
desire to stop drinking/using	
on probation for two years: required to stay clean	
learning a new set of coping skills from therapist	
practices yoga/works out (runs)	
several friends, nonusers outside of meetings	
SSRI seems to help mood overall	

A worksheet like this may actually surprise a client by how many qualities are in the assets column. Similarly, a client may find herself surprised by how much is in the debits column, which can motivate her to begin working on building assets. Justin's sample list illustrates two important elements to consider about this idea of recovery capital. First, just about anything a person can use to stay sober qualifies as an asset, be it internal or external, tangible or intangible. Justin's list includes both external motivations (e.g., probation, relationship with nieces and nephews) and internal motivations (e.g., the desire to stay sober). Moreover, it includes tangible resources (e.g., insurance, transportation) and intangible resources (e.g., family support). Take everything into consideration.

The second element is that no one program, treatment center, or modality appears in the assets column of the list. For Justin, a twelve-step sponsor and meetings fit the bill, but for others, it may be a church support group or another recovery program. The essential principle here is to call upon anything you can access to build the assets side of the list and make sure that, through your time working together, it becomes longer than the debits list.

If a person is willing, you can also take this exercise a step further by having him identify opportunities for turning the debits into assets. For instance, Justin has no job for the time being. There are several opportunities here. One, as a counselor or helper, you can work with him on some vocational and investigation skills to help him find work. Two, you can emphasize that since he is not currently employed, that frees up time for him to go to more meetings and to schedule his therapy appointments without conflict. In looking at some of his issues with enabling or people who otherwise drink or use in his life, there are multiple opportunities there for Justin to build upon his skills in assertiveness and coping.

The anthem of teaching solid sets of coping skills that I have harped on in this book has a clear place in helping a client build recovery capital, especially if a client comes to treatment with few items in the assets column. Little external recovery capital should not be called upon as an excuse as to why a person cannot get sober or why trauma cannot be addressed. It simply means that you, as the helper, will need to assist your client in *building* capital as part of his trauma-informed treatment plan, and teaching him a solid arsenal of coping skills can help with this task. Consider the case of Judy (adapted from my book *EMDR Made Simple*):

The Case of Judy

Judy, a lower-income Caucasian woman in her late thirties, found herself in and out of community mental health facilities for the better part of her adult life. She suffered from both bipolar disorder and PTSD, resulting from a series of abuses at the hands of her alcoholic parents and sexual assaults in late adolescence. Although Judy never received a diagnosis of a substance dependence disorder, she reported periods of substance abuse throughout her adult life to cope with stress, usually when she was not compliant with her medications for the bipolar disorder. She struggled significantly with medication compliance. Although medication regulated her bipolar symptoms, she often complained about the side effects and cost of the medications.

Judy presented to a community treatment center that offered several therapeutic options for cathartic trauma work (e.g., EMDR, trauma-focused CBT, Gestalt therapy). Her therapist initially did not consider Judy a candidate for any of these therapies because she seemed so unstable. Judy was adamant that if she just got on the right medication, all her problems would go away. During the first two months of treatment, Judy's therapist was careful to meet her where she was and not use overt confrontation, even about behaviors that were clearly detrimental to her mental health progress (e.g., choosing certain friends, attempting to reason with her equally troubled ex-husband). As a result, a solid alliance formed. Through some trial and error, Judy's psychiatrist was able to find a medication that worked well in keeping the bipolar symptoms reasonably stabilized, and the level of Judy's day-to-day lability significantly decreased.

During these first couple of months, Judy's therapist worked with her on coping skills, including guided imagery and deep breathing. Judy responded well to these two exercises, so her therapist suggested they try adding some tactile coping skill elements, like pressure points and bilateral tapping. Judy's therapist explained the tapping as a process that might help to further enhance her relaxation. They worked on a light stream guided imagery technique, together with some tactile stimulation, and Judy reported that she felt more relaxed than ever before. During the next session, the therapist taught Judy a guided imagery safe place exercise using bilateral stimulation, and Judy reported that she liked that exercise as well. For the next few months, Judy and her therapist engaged in a virtual boot camp of body-based coping skills training. Because Judy did not have much good going on in her life, aside from receiving a government housing apartment and having solid relationships with her case manager and therapist, building resources became incredibly important.

The therapist, after seeing how well Judy responded to the coping skill exercises, explained how they could use the stimulation in a different way to help process some of the traumatic memories. Judy was game. The first several sessions of trauma processing with the EMDR modality were all over the place in terms of tangential disorganization. However, after these first several sessions, Judy was able to quickly reprocess a series of traumatic memories that were both recent (an accident) and deep seated (past abuse). Judy and her therapist used EMDR off and on over a nine-month period (breaks in EMDR occurred because during some sessions Judy stated a need to just talk), which led to significant improvements in Judy's overall self-image and decision-making.

If the cathartic trauma reprocessing began too quickly, especially with someone presenting with as many complications as Judy did, more harm would have resulted. It was important to introduce coping skills slowly and carefully, then add the bilateral stimulation, and then proceed with trauma reprocessing. Prepare for the journey, and the journey will go much more smoothly.

Yoga

Yoga is an ancient practice that originated in India. Roughly translated, the word *yoga* means "union." A series of breathing techniques, stretches, poses, and meditative qualities designed to promote integration between the body, mind, and spirit, yoga has become an increasingly popular addition to gym-class schedules in recent years. Despite the billion-dollar industry of yoga apparel, videos, and classes that have sprung up, yoga's potential as a healing art is what makes it of utmost interest to many recovering individuals. Because its integrative properties are vast, yoga is excellent at helping a person master the healing power of his breath while, at the same time, helping a person to better get in touch with his body and its subtle cues. In my view, a person well guided in her initial steps into yoga practice, has the perfect treatment support for integrated trauma recovery.

Many treatment centers now offer yoga as part of their programming, and some community yoga schools are now offering their version of "twelve-step" yoga classes that integrate twelve-step spiritual principles in with yoga practice. Even without these specialty classes, a person working a recovery program can benefit from standard yoga classes that the community offers. It is generally important for a new student of yoga, especially one in recovery, to talk to a yoga teacher at a local school or gym first to make sure that the class is appropriate for the student. Sometimes, people get repulsed by yoga when they're put into a "power" or "hot" yoga class, when what their body (and their recovery) most needs at the moment is a gentle or restorative yoga class. Although yoga is excellent for stage-one stabilization work, it also has the potential to bring up material that is grist for the mill in stage two, trauma reprocessing. Thus, it is important to know that they are practicing yoga in a safe place with an instructor who may be aware of their emotional concerns about yoga practice. I often encourage clients of mine who are going to try yoga for the first time to talk to an instructor via phone or e-mail before attending a class.

I highly recommend the excellent book *Overcoming Trauma through Yoga: Reclaiming Your Body* by David Emerson and Elizabeth Hopper (2011). This book offers an excellent primer on yoga practice for professionals and potential recovering yoga students, and it lists some modifications that those in trauma recovery may consider. Another outstanding book on using trauma as a recovering resource is Amy Weintraub's (2004) *Yoga and Depression* and her newest book, *Yoga Skills for Therapists* (2012).

CHAPTER 10

Strategies for Reprocessing and Reintegration

In working with addiction professionals as colleagues, and having contact with numerous others at my workshops over the years, there is one line I always hear that seems to sum up their resistance to doing trauma work: "I just don't want to go somewhere with them before they're ready to handle it…what if they relapse?" The concern is legitimate. Opening up the Pandora's box of past traumas may destabilize a person, perhaps even leading him to relapse, if proper stabilization is not in place. However, I am not advocating that professionals, or even recovery sponsors, encourage a person to examine and process her traumatic experiences before she is ready. The answer is not to have a person who is still actively using, or in her second day of detox, go through deep regression work on past traumas. As I have emphasized throughout this book, stabilization is essential before moving into the interventions that we discuss in this chapter.

A common question always surfaces: When can clients, especially ones with addiction issues, move from the stabilization stage of treatment into the reprocessing stage, where they are more likely to do the cathartic work? Although this is a question with no finite answer, we ask series of questions on a case-by-case basis to help evaluate whether or not a client is ready to move from stabilization to reprocessing. Using these guidelines can also help us to evaluate how well we are helping a client build her individualized recovery capital:

- *Have I assessed for secondary gains?*

Secondary gains are what a person "gets" out of staying sick or otherwise stuck in his symptoms. These gains can be as tangible as a government disability check or as subtle as maintaining an excuse for irresponsible behavior because of the diagnosis. ("Well, it's the PTSD acting up.") I usually approach this issue with clients as directly as possible. If they seem to be clinging to reasons for staying stuck in maladaptive behavior, I talk about it with them in the context of our therapeutic alliance. Traditional addiction counseling often refers to this process as calling a person out on their behavior. Essentially, I endorse this idea, as long as it happens after establishing rapport and we target the behavior without belittling the person in question.

- *What is the client's motivation for wanting to do trauma-processing work?*

I am hesitant to do any trauma processing work with a client when the reason given for seeking treatment is "to find out why I am the way I am" or "to find out why I drink/use." I am especially hesitant to do this with an addict if she has made no effort to embrace lifestyle change, and she feels that a simple explanation for her problems lies in the past. In the spirit of safety, I will not do trauma processing work unless I am reasonably convinced that a client bases her motivations for doing so on getting well and not ascribing blame to others or finding "magic" answers. All trauma reprocessing therapies may reveal some clues from the past, but I make sure a client knows that it's what she does with those clues that matters (Marich, 2011).

- *Does the client understand what may happen if change results and the effects of the trauma on his or her life start to shift?*

If trauma reprocessing works for the client, he may genuinely change and resultantly adopt healthier lifestyle patterns. Discuss this with a client ahead of time to make sure he's aware of this potential, especially if people in his life are used to him being sick or unhealthy (which is often the case in addicted family dynamics).

- *Does the client have emotional support resources, including, but not limited to, an AA sponsor, home group and support network, church group, and access to healthy and easily accessible friends and family?*

Simply put, if the client has an emotionally draining counseling session and has some distur-bance after she goes home, is there someone healthy and supportive, besides you, whom your client can call? I encourage clients to let at least one person in their life know they are going through intense counseling about traumatic issues in their past before we begin cathartic work. The absence of a support system does not necessarily rule out such therapy with a client. It does mean that you must spend more time preparing. If the client is genuinely without any positive social support, explore whether there are twenty-four-hour on-call services in your community or ask yourself whether you would be willing to be contacted more regularly via your answering service during this client's trauma processing (Marich, 2011).

- *Is the client able to reasonably calm and/or relax himself or herself when distressed?*

The client does not have to be able to perfectly calm himself down when distressed…if he could, your services probably would not be necessary! Ask these simple questions in your evaluation: Can he use one or more coping skills to self-soothe? Do I have reasonable assurance that my cli-ent can and does use these skills outside of session? I always have clients test out, on their own time, the coping skills and affect regulation exercises on which we have worked together before I proceed with trauma processing.

- *Is there a sufficient amount of adaptive, healthy material in the client's life?*

This is the classic *recovery capital* question…adaptive, healthy material can include everything from acquisition of the basic needs (e.g., food, water, shelter) to work, hobbies, a supportive family, life goals, and healthy friends. The absence of such positive material does not rule out reproc-essing work, but it does necessitate more advanced preparation in the realm of recovery capital.

A Caution

There are many professionals out there who may be scandalized to read that I am even including this chapter in a book that many non-professionals, like 12-step sponsors, are likely to pick up. I have heard the criticism, "But someone may pick this book up and try these strategies without any training or supervision." Although I am not advocating that lay people, or even therapists, engage in any *specialty* interventions that I have listed in this chapter without the proper training, I do not feel that some of the basics of trauma processing need to be kept in the dark since the reality is, many good 12-step sponsors are already assisting or completing some of the tasks of trauma processing. Wise folks throughout the centuries were helping people process trauma long before professional psychotherapy even existed. And as far as the danger of people picking up a book and thinking they're a therapist, I am not the first one to introduce that risk; simply having books written by therapists available on Amazon.com for anyone to order introduced this risk long before my book came to be.

So my caution is to proceed with caution. If you know you're over your head when it comes to these strategies, either due to a lack of training or a lack of competency when it comes to under-standing trauma and how to handle it, seek help. There is no shame, ever, in asking for help or admitting when you're over your head. That's what recovery is about, right?

Trauma Reprocessing

Every professional must make a personal judgment call, based on her training, experience, and comfort with trauma work, about whether or not she feels qualified to work with the addicted client with unresolved trauma on the reprocessing, or cathartic, piece of the trauma work. As a trauma-addiction specialist, a question I get all the time is what qualifies a professional to really work with trauma in addicted individuals. I try to assure clinicians that if they are considering the broadest possible definition of trauma, it is likely that they have already engaged in reprocess-ing work with a client, whether they realize it or not. That being said, in order to effectively do reprocessing activities with an addicted survivor of trauma, you must be personally comfortable with trauma and the sheer horror of material that may surface, ensuring that you have addressed enough of your own issues to stay present and not "freak out" on the client. You must also have a similar level of comfort with addiction and be willing to demonstrate most of the Rogerian qualities that we discussed in the previous chapter. If you have created an environment of safety and flexibility in your therapeutic setting, and if you have also allowed for adequate stabilization, then, in my view, you will be able to work with a client on reprocessing, implementing the skills and techniques you are comfortable using in practice.

In this section of the chapter, we discuss relatively simple strategies that you can implement for trauma reprocessing using the existing skill sets that most clinicians possess. Then, we discuss other specialized modalities as options for referral. The scope of this book does not allow detailed explanation of each modality; moreover, many of these specialized modalities require advanced training. However, this section will familiarize you with what you need to know about how these specialty services may help the people you work with and how you can best access them as capital for your clients.

One of the primary principles of effective trauma reprocessing is to find which approach to it will work best for the individual client. Some people need to be able to tell the story in great detail to be able to connect the cognitive pieces of their trauma with the emotional and somatic pieces in order for full resolution to occur. For others, speaking the story in great detail simply generates too much distress, and writing may be a better option. Others may work out the distress on the yoga mat or out in nature for this integration to occur, and still others may utilize a combination of all of these elements. The main point to keep in mind is that there is no one right way to help a client reprocess trauma. Effectiveness in this area is really a matter of meeting a person where she is *at* with a variety of options or tasks that she can engage in to allow for resolution and integration.

Toolkit Strategy: Finding What Works

In order to help your client identify which modalities will best help her reprocess her traumatic experiences, it is first helpful for you as the professional to reflect upon what has worked for you to reprocess in the past. Think about something in your life, be it a significant life transition or a major trauma. In your reflection, what really helped you to work through it to obtain some sort of functional resolution? Was it one modality or activity, or a combination?

Consider how the information you obtained in your reflection above may give you some insight into how your clients work. There is a worksheet in the appendix that you can use with your clients to help them evaluate what may work the best for their trauma reprocessing experience.

Telling the story. There are a variety of ways for a person to tell the story of his trauma that can lead toward resolution. As the case of Jeff demonstrated in chapter 4, for some, being able to share their stories over and over again at twelve-step meetings until the major emotional charge in the stories lessens is one way to use storytelling as a method of reprocessing. Others find similar healing in fourth- and fifth-step work. There are some who may never feel optimally comfortable sharing the story in front of a group of people, so writing it down, either literally or through the use of fiction and allegory, is an option. I once had a client who wrote an entire novel about his traumatic experience, changing certain names and situations while exaggerating other elements for dramatic effect. Yet as I read his work, it was clear to me that he used the story as a way of creating a new, more desired ending for himself that helped him move on from the trauma. In certain African cultures, speaking about the exact details of a trauma is taboo, yet using allegory—specifically animals as characters—is a more than acceptable manner of telling the story for the purpose of catharsis.

Songwriting and other performance elements, like dance and the visual arts, are other outstanding ways to tell the story for the purposes of resolution. If you listen to the work of many singer-songwriters who have battled the demons of addiction and trauma in their lives, it is clear how they have used their songwriting craft to reprocess many of their experiences. Neil Young's "The Needle and the Damage Done" and Stevie Nicks's "Landslide" are two of my favorite examples of this phenomenon. Many dance forms exist that can help individuals use movement as a way to tell their story and experience emotional cleansing. If you are interested in exploring the various dance forms that can help with this process and how to access them in your area, consider checking out the publication and website *Conscious Dancer* (www.consciousdancer.com); they also have a Facebook page with resources. Many videos on dance forms are available online, such as *JourneyDance*™, *Biodanza*,® *Shake Your Soul*®, *Soulmotion*™, *5Rhythms*®, *Nia*®, and *Let Your Yoga Dance*®, clearly demonstrating that, for some, integrative storytelling best happens through movement. Considered by many to be a conscious dance form, *Zumba*® (best described as a Latin dance workout) is a popular class offering at many gyms around the world. Many people report emotional, as well as physical benefits from the workout.

In the psychotherapeutic setting, an individual may simply need you as a guide to tell her story over a period of sessions. The basic logic behind trauma-focused cognitive behavioral therapy is that it is not enough to simply confront a person's negative beliefs about herself. Rather, the origins of such beliefs must be explored, and doing this within a supportive therapeutic context through which you as the professional hear the client tell his story can be what many clients need to heal.

The art of using storytelling as a method of trauma reprocessing was professionally systemized into an approach called narrative therapy. Although information is available on how to use the art of storytelling with more finesse and refinement, specifically in the landmark work *Narrative Means to Therapeutic Ends* (White, 2000), I typically caution clinicians and sponsors alike not to overcomplicate matters. Many people coming to us for help simply need us to hear them, and we can accomplish this task using a variety of basic therapeutic methods in combination with some good old-fashioned common sense.

Classic Gestalt methods: Empty chair and unsent letter. Addiction treatment often incorporates two methods from the Gestalt tradition of psychotherapy: the *empty chair* technique and the *unsent letter* technique. When used properly within the context of adequate stabilization, both are excellent for trauma processing. In the empty chair technique, an individual literally imagines the person who abused or traumatized him in an empty chair. Then, the client says everything to that person that he needs to get off his chest. Sometimes, empty chair sessions can be very emotional, eliciting the necessary screams, wails, and tears that a person may have been holding in for decades.

A similar technique, and one of my personal favorites to use within formal therapy and informally with twelve-step recovering peers is the unsent letter. There are numerous variations on the unsent letter technique; the key is to find which variation or combination of variations will work best for a specific client. The basic premise of the unsent letter is that a person writes out everything he or she would like to say to the abuser/person who caused the trauma. When I encourage people to do this, I emphasize that the intention is not to send this letter (at least the initial draft of it), but rather to get out everything that needs to come out. I encourage people to write uncensored—swear, curse, lash out—just get out all of the feelings that they have held in. Case in point: when I did an unsent letter several years back to deal with unfinished business about someone, I must have dropped about ten F-bombs on each page!

After a person writes the first letter, you can collaboratively decide what would be most healing. For instance, some people find comfort in taking the letter to a gravesite in the case of a deceased abuser. Other people may take great joy in ripping the letter up, feeling the physical sensations as they tear the pages and throw them away. Very often, my clients do this in my office and dump the torn pages in my wastebasket, symbolizing that they are letting the material go and leaving it behind in the office. Many people find great spiritual significance in going outside and burning the pages, watching the smoke rise to the sky as a symbol of ultimate release to some entity that is greater than the individual. When I wrote my profanity-laced letter, I actually put it in the prayer intentions bin at a local church (I knew that this church burns the intentions after a few weeks); for me, it symbolized turning my pain over to my Higher Power. Once again, the options and combinations are endless.

Some people like to write one letter to the same person each week or each month until they feel that the issue has resolved and they can try to embrace some semblance of forgiveness. One time, a client of mine wrote one letter each week to her deceased mother. She found that with each week, the level of anger dissipated, and by the end of six weeks, she had arrived at a place of loving acceptance about her mother's life and the pain that her mother caused her.

Another option involves the writer imagining what the response to the letters might be. After writing the unsent letter, the client writes two letters back to himself from the point of view of the abuser—one letter represents the words that the client would *like* to hear from the abuser, and the other letter contains the words with which the abuser would *likely* respond. Then, you can have the client notice her reactions and feelings after reading each letter.

One question naturally arises as we explore empty chair and unsent letter: Should the client ever really confront the abuser face-to-face or should she ever send the letter? Of course, opinions vary about this matter. I tend to embrace the recovery logic that we, as people, can drive ourselves crazy when we try to reason with a crazy person! Thus, I typically find confronting the abuser or actually sending the letters to be fruitless efforts unless the client has the express understanding that she the abuser will likely ignore, stonewall, or further demean her. Some people, knowing the risks, still feel that they need to engage in this confrontation for their own resolution, and I generally support this if adequate stabilization and recovery basics are in place. However, in most cases, I feel that the empty chair or unsent letter techniques provide elegant, safe alternatives that typically yield just as much, or even more good, than if a person actually engaged in confrontation or sending the letter.

Cognitive behavioral therapies. Cognitive behavioral therapies seem to be the "gold standard" that most therapists in this current generation have been trained to use as part of standard practice. The whole logic of change the thoughts, change the behavior seems to make good sense to scores of practitioners. However, as we have amply covered in this book, there are limitations to cognitive behavioral approaches because the part of the brain that is most used during cognitive interventions (the neocortex) tends to get paralyzed when the person is activated by traumatic stimuli in the limbic brain.

This does not mean that we have to abandon cognitive-behavioral interventions as part of trauma-sensitive reprocessing, but it does mean that we need to modify them with simple, body-based approaches and sensitivity to the role that the past plays. As I heard early on in my recovery, "It is better to act your way into better thinking than to think your way into better acting." This simple axiom encapsulates the spirit of trauma-sensitive addiction treatment. Learning to engage in healthier behaviors and embracing action-oriented coping skills, topics addressed throughout this book, effectively and adaptively affects a person's thinking. Thus, if you are primarily a cognitive-behavioral therapist, you can use many of your existing techniques to help a client reprocess her traumas, as long as you bring the body into the process. Many call this general approach *mindfulness-based cognitive therapy.*

Another approach often credited as being effective in helping people reprocess is *trauma-focused cognitive-behavioral therapy*. As the name suggests, in this approach, we are concerned with helping clients go back to the traumatic origins of their negative schema. For instance, if a person's core negative belief is "I am unlovable," asking the relevant questions, like "When did you first start believing that?" and "What happened in your past to give you that belief?" are critical so that we can help that person reprocess those experiences. Of course, this differs from other cognitive approaches, like reality therapy/choice theory and rational emotive behavioral therapy, in which the aim is to stay in the here and now, avoiding lengthy discussions about the past. The trauma-focused cognitive approach acknowledges the biological reality that a person with unresolved trauma may find it virtually impossible to stay in the here and now because of the past; so naturally, he must explore, examine, and reprocess to instill healthier cognitive schema.

Specialty therapies requiring additional training. Remember, when it comes to reprocessing traumatic experiences in survivors, what works best for the client is what works. There is no magic bullet or instant answer that I or anyone else can give you (and if someone claims to have the magic answer, be very skeptical). If some of the approaches I have explored thus far in this chapter are not working for your clients, there are a plethora of other action-oriented, integrated approaches to healing that may prove useful in reprocessing traumatic experiences in the quest toward reintegration with healthy life functioning. Any clinician can use these suggested interventions based on existing training, some fundamental knowledge about trauma, and willingness to examine the clinician's own issues with trauma and intense affect.

In this section, I present other options for reprocessing. These approaches require additional training for safe and responsible execution. I am not saying that you need to receive training in all of these; however, you may find your interest to receive additional training piqued. I have provided some web-based resources where you can read more about each therapy and find listings of providers in your local area. My best encouragement to you is to spend time exploring; if possible, network in your local community and talk to someone who provides one of these specialty treatments. Learn about what they do, and talk to them about whether or not they have found their approach to be effective in working with addicted individuals. Although I do not specifically endorse any of the approaches listed here—as I've proclaimed throughout the book, what might work great for one person may not be the best fit for another—I do feel that all of these approaches are potentially good fits for individuals who have maximized their benefit from traditional, talk-therapy methods. All of these approaches are excellent at offering an integrated element—bringing the body, mind, and spirit into the process. The key is helping a client find a modality that is most agreeable to his or her sensibilities and interests.

Possible Modalities for Reprocessing

APPROACH	RECOMMENDED WEBSITES
Accelerated Experiential Dynamic Psychotherapy	http://www.aedpinstitute.org
Acceptance and Commitment Therapy	http://contextualpsychology.org/act
Art Therapy	http://www.playtherapy.org
	http://www.internationalarttherapy.org
Brainspotting	http://www.brainspotting.pro
Coherence Therapy	http://www.coherencetherapy.org/
The Developmental Needs Meeting Strategy	http://www.dnmsinstitute.com
Emotional Freedom Techniques	http://www.energypsych.org
Equine Assisted Therapy	http://www.pathintl.org/
	http://www.equine-therapy-programs.com/
Eye Movement Desensitization and Reprocessing (EMDR)	http://www.emdrinfo.com
	http://www.emdr.com
	http://www.emdrinaction.com
	http://www.trauma101.com
Energy Psychology	http://www.energypsych.org
Exposure Therapy	http://www.ptsd.va.gov/public/pages/prolonged-exposure-therapy.asp
Focusing	http://www.focusing.org
Gestalt Therapy	http://www.gestalt.org
	http://www.gestalttherapy.net
Hakomi	http://www.hakomiinstitute.com

Hypnosis & Hypnotherapy	http://www.hypnosis.org
	http://www.asch.net
Internal Family Systems Therapy	http://www.selfleadership.org
Neuro Emotional Technique (NET)	http://www.netmindbody.com
Neurofeedback	http://www.isnr.org
Neurolinguistic Programming (NLP)	http://www.neurolinguisticprogramming.com
Play Therapy	http://www.a4pt.org/
	http://www.playtherapy.org/
Psychoanalysis	http://www.apsa.org
Psychodrama	http://www.asgpp.org/pdrama1.html
	http://www.nccata.org/psychodrama.html
Sensorimotor Psychology	http://www.sensorimotorpsychotherapy.org
Somatic Experiencing	http://www.somaticexperiencing.com
Stress Inoculation	https://www.ptsdforum.org/c/wiki/stress-inoculation-therapy/
Systematic desensitization	http://www.ptsd.va.gov/public/pages/prolonged-exposure-therapy.asp
Yoga Therapy	http://www.iayt.org/

This list is not exhaustive. Many healing forms offer promise in helping a recovering person to reprocess trauma. Some have more research basis than others do. Some present themselves with a more entrepreneurial slant than others, punctuated with a variety of trademark symbols and extensive training programs in the method. Others are rooted in more traditional psychotherapeutic techniques. The key is to find out what works for the individual person along her recovery journey.

So What Is Evidence Anyway?

You hear the term "evidenced-based" tossed around conversations in the addiction and psychology fields quite a bit. What constitutes *good evidence*? Some people want to see a rigorous standard of randomized controlled research studies that meet some organization's recipe for a "standard" before they accept something as evidenced-based, and others (like me), see these types of research studies and standards as out-of-touch with what goes on in the real world. While I am much more the type of therapist who values what several of my patients have coined as helpful over any published study when I'm defining evidence, I am aware that many professionals might look at the list I provided in "Possible Modalities for Trauma Processing" and tell me that Organization X , Standard Y, or Insurance Company Q does not deem this practice as "evidenced based" in treating trauma and addiction concurrently. My best guidance is to use your judgment based on the setting you practice and on what you know, in your gut, to be true about human nature. Yes, some of these practices have more research base than others, but ever the self-proclaimed "clinical folk academic," this chapter contains what I know has worked for more than one person on more than one occasion.

My favorite organizational definition of what constitutes an evidence-based treatment comes from the American Psychological Association (2006): an *evidence-based practice* in psychology is "the best available research with clinical expertise in the context of patient characteristics, culture, and preferences." You can also check out the website of the Substance Abuse and Mental Health Services Administration (SAMHSA), available at www.samhsa.gov for a complete listing of what that organization considers to be "evidenced based" practices, or the emerging "promising practices" based on their research standards.

Then again, if petting a horse or working with animals helped you to overcome your trauma in a truly holistic manner, that may be all the evidence that you personally need, right? Like with so many things in this field and in discussions about recovery, defining "evidence" often depends on who you ask.

My Story...Continued

Throughout this book, I have shared with you some candid reflections on my own recovery journey. From my childhood upbringing to the orange trailer in Bosnia, it has certainly been an extraordinary process. In writing this book on a topic for which I have great passion, I have been forced to look back at what worked for me the most during my recovery journey, and the key is that no one element, no one magic bullet, no singular, *voila!* therapy helped me instantly heal my legacy of trauma. Too often, we pick up books as professionals in the field seeking that instant answer. What I have found is that no *instant answer* exists. Rather, integration of approaches and meeting people where they are *at* in the recovery journey are key.

For me, a combination of having my traumatic experiences validated, having a trauma-sensitive provider care for me, and going to meetings early on are what helped me get sober. Really digging in and doing a lot of self-discovery with journal writing, songwriting, and "stepwork" are what helped me stay sober. Doing EMDR therapy at around two to three years of sobriety is what helped free me from many of my mental burdens, helping me transition from victim to survivor. Engaging in bodywork (like cranial-sacral massage, aromatherapy, and hydrotherapy) helped me to enhance my self-care potential as an addicted survivor of trauma working as a professional. In recent years, continuing to write, perform music, dance, practice yoga, and engage in a few other therapeutic techniques like NET and coherence therapy have helped me move from survivor to *thriver*, all while staying in touch with the relationship I've fostered with my Higher Power. One of my dearest support figures in recovery, a wise woman named Denise, often tells me, "Jamie, addiction is one disease where, in our recovery, we choose how *well* we want to get."

I couldn't agree more. Because of my history of trauma and emotional vulnerabilities, I have had to seek a variety of outlets for stabilization, reprocessing, and reintegration—that has worked for me and I'm grateful. One time, early on in my recovery, I was sharing my healing ventures with my brother Paul: going to meetings, going to therapy, going to church, going for massage, writing music, and performing it with my partner. He jokingly said, "It takes a village to help my sister." Although he and I laugh about this comment today, it is a true observation—one that I feel has helped me to thrive. I hope that more people working twelve-step recovery programs, especially those who have histories of trauma, can embrace this mentality in order to attain optimal wellness. My story of trauma-addiction recovery is a book that I continue to write. It has been a privilege to share with you some of my story in this book, and I hope that as I connect with readers, clients, and workshop attendees, I will have even more opportunities to hear about what has worked for you in your recovery journey.

From Reprocessing to Reintegration

The word *integration* seems to best encapsulate the ultimate goal of reprocessing trauma. Through integration, one brings together parts of an experience that were once disjointed and chaotic and helps them fit together in a way that makes sense. Engaging in such a process may finally bring a recovering individual to a place where he or she is able to live life *one day at a time*. Engaging in such a process and having an integrated sense of wholeness emerge where the debris of scattered emotional shards once existed can help a person to truly heal from and move past the wounds of the past, embracing a lifestyle of recovery and wellness.

In the consensus model of trauma treatment, the third stage, reintegration, implies that we, as human beings, were born with an innate sense of wholeness and an ability to contribute to society at large. Engaging in the healing work of stabilization and trauma processing restores a person to his birthright. It is important that we, as helpers, not just leave a person to fend for himself or herself after reprocessing the trauma. As I explained in *EMDR Made Simple* (2011; p. 266), "An emotional burden is like a heavy backpack filled with rocks and other items, all of which weigh a person down, but when someone has been living with such a burden for months, years, or even decades, as painful and as bothersome as it may be, he or she may find some way, even if it's maladaptive, to carry that weight a long time (with credit to John Lennon and Paul McCartney for the song lyric)." Thus, professionals and recovery sponsors have a duty to help a person through the process of readjusting to life without the weight.

Toolkit Strategy: The Adjustment of Reintegration

Think about one of your current clients on your caseload, or someone you may work with in recovery. Let's say that the chosen person goes through the essential work of reprocessing his or her traumatic experience(s). What next? What are some of the adjustments a person may need your help to deal with? What strategies we've covered in the book thus far may prove helpful?

If there's one note that I hope to have sung throughout this book, it's that helping a person in addiction recovery heal from the aftereffects of trauma does not have to be rocket science. Simple knowledge of how trauma affects a person, awareness of our own issues connected to trauma and addiction, attention to relational imperatives, and willingness to incorporate the entire being into treatment (body, mind, and spirit) are the keys. Carrying these essential guidelines into the reintegration process is no different. Adjustment, even positive adjustment, can cause its own share of stressors. However, what you *do* to help a person in the stabilization stage, especially paying attention to the healing quality of a relationship, has just as much impact in the reintegration stage. It really all does come full circle.

Handouts & Resources

Use the tools in this section at your own clinical discretion. They are encapsulations of several skills and techniques covered in this book. Feel free to copy them and use them as needed in your settings. Most of the handouts are self-explanatory, and you can refer back to the pertinent sections in the book for further explanation.

The first set of handouts is primarily for screening. By giving them to a client, you can help him identify his areas of strength as well as what roadblocks to wellness you need to address as part of a trauma-sensitive treatment plan.

Handout 1: *The "Greatest Hits List" of Positive Affirmations*—Give this list to a client and have him check off any positive beliefs he holds about himself. Even if it's just one or two beliefs, you can still use these for resource building (e.g., incorporate into positive affirmations and discussion about positive/empowering memories, useful for guided imageries)

Handouts 2 and 3: *The "Greatest Hits List" of Problematic Beliefs* and *The "Greatest Hits List" of Problematic Addiction-Specific Beliefs*—These are largely resources that will help you identify how trauma and addiction have subjectively affected a person, informing you how to best direct the treatment plan. General instructions for use:

Give the client the respective list (you may choose to have the client complete the list at home or in your office).

Advise the client to read the negative list and to check off any belief that she still considers a problem. Assure the client that there are no wrong answers: one item, ten items, or all items may be checked.

If more than one item is checked, ask the client to rank the two to three most problematic beliefs.

Go through each of the top two or three items and ask the client:

"When's the first time you ever remember getting that message about yourself?"

"When's the worst time you ever remember getting that message about yourself?"

"When's the most recent time you received that message about yourself?"

The second set of handouts will help clients identify their strengths, resources, and recovery capital that can contribute to their overall plan of wellness. Once again, it is at your clinical discretion whether you want to work on these handouts with clients or have clients do the work on their own.

Handout 4: *Wound Care 101: Planning Your Treatment*—This worksheet gives clients a visual overview of the three-stage consensus model of trauma treatment that will help them better see the general direction of a trauma-sensitive treatment plan.

Handout 5: *Assets and Debits Column*—Explained in chapter 9, this handout encourages clients to list their assets (the tangible and intangible resources they have going for the service of their recovery) and debits (the roadblocks, tangible or intangible, standing in the way of overall wellness).

Handout 6: *Finding Where I Most Belong*—This worksheet will help clients take an inventory of the various recovery meetings they are exploring as part of their recovery. Clients are encouraged to reflect on what they liked about the meeting, what they didn't like about the meeting, what trauma triggers may have been set off by the meeting or group, and what, if anything, they did to help them get through any problems at the meeting.

Handout 7: *What May Work Best for Me*—This worksheet asks clients to self-examine both their traumatic issues that need resolution and their tastes in learning styles and activities. Together, this will help you and the client figure out which methods might work best for processing.

The "Greatest Hits" List of Positive Affirmations

Developed by Jamie Marich, PhD

(May be duplicated for use in clinical settings)

<u>Responsibility</u>

I did the best I could.

I do the best I can with what I have.

I did/do my best.

I am not at fault.

I can be trusted.

<u>Safety</u>

I can trust myself.

I can choose who to trust.

I am safe now.

I can create my sense of safety.

I can show my emotions.

<u>Power</u>

I am in control.

I have power now.

I can help myself.

I have a way out.

I have options.

I can get what I want.

I can succeed.

I can stand up for myself.

I can let it out.

<u>Value</u>

I am good enough.

I am a good person.

I am whole.

I am blessed.

I am unique.

I am worthy.

I am significant.

I am important.

I deserve to live.

I deserve only good things.

I am smart.

I can belong.

I am special.

I am a success.

I am beautiful.

My body is sacred.

I can make friends.

It's OK to make mistakes.

I can only please myself.

I cannot please everyone.

Others Not Listed:

The "Greatest Hits" List of Problematic Beliefs

Developed by Jamie Marich, PhD

(May be duplicated for use in clinical settings)

Responsibility

I should have known better.

I should have done something.

I did something wrong.

I am to blame.

I cannot be trusted.

I am worthless/inadequate.

Safety

I cannot trust myself.

I cannot trust anyone.

I am in danger.

I am not safe.

I cannot show my emotions.

I am different.

Choice

I am not in control.

I have to be perfect/please everyone.

I am weak.

I am trapped.

I have no options.

Power

I cannot get what I want.

I cannot succeed.

I cannot stand up for myself.

I cannot let it out.

I am powerless/helpless.

Value

I am not good enough.

I am a bad person.

I am permanently damaged.

I am defective.

I am terrible.

I am insignificant.

I am not important.

I deserve to die.

I deserve only bad things.

I am stupid.

I do not belong.

I am a failure.

I am ugly.

My body is ugly.

I am alone.

The "Greatest Hits" List of Addiction-Specific Beliefs

Developed by Jamie Marich, PhD

(May be duplicated for use in clinical settings)

My addiction is my security.

I cannot cope without alcohol.

I cannot cope without cigarettes.

I cannot cope without drugs.

I cannot cope without victimizing others.

I cannot accept/deal with reality.

I cannot cope without acting out violently.

I cannot live without sex.

I cannot cope with emotions without eating.

I cannot survive without a partner/relationship.

I must use alcohol to cope with my past.

I must eat to be in control.

I must act out violently to cope with my past.

I must victimize others to cope with my past.

I must gamble to be in control.

I must drink alcohol to be in control.

I must use drugs to be in control.

I must smoke cigarettes to cope with my past.

I am not capable of dealing with my life.

I must smoke cigarettes to be in control.

I must act out violently to be in control.

I must victimize others to be in control.

I must be in a relationship to be in control.

I must have sex to be in control.

I must use drugs to cope with my past.

I must eat to cope with my past.

I must have sex to cope with my past.

I have no identity without my addiction.

I have no identity if I can't act out.

I am not capable of dealing with my feelings.

I am incapable of being social without alcohol.

I am incapable of being social without drugs.

I am incapable of being social without cigarettes.

Food is my most important need.

Alcohol is my most important need.

Drugs are my most important need.

Gambling is my most important need.

Violence is my most important need.

Sex is my most important need.

Escaping reality is my most important need.

Others Not Listed:

Wound Care 101: Planning Your Treatment

STEP 1: Bandaging the Wounds

<u>Useful Coping Skills</u>   <u>When to Use This Skill</u>

STEP 2: Looking Beneath the Surface

<u>Issues I Will Need to Work on to Reach My Goals</u>

STEP 3: Total Healing

<u>What My Life Will Look Like after I've Done the Healing Work</u>

Recovery Capital: Assets and Debits

Assets:

<u>What I Have "Going for Me" In Recovery</u>

Debits:

<u>What's Working against Me in Recovery</u>

Finding Where I Most Belong:

A Log of My Recovery Meeting Experiences

Meeting and Date	Likes	Dislikes	Triggers	What Helped to Address Any Triggers

What Works Best for Me

What are some of the issues I know I need to "get over," especially about my past, in order to stay sober and be well?

In the past, these things, people, or activities have helped me deal with extreme emotional pain:

Some of my favorite coping skills include:

Tying all of this together, my gut tells me that the following plan might work best for helping me get over the past issues:

References

Adler, A. (1931). What life could mean to you. In Stein, H. T. (Ed.), *The collected works of Alfred Adler* (Vol. 6). Bellingham, WA: The Alfred Adler Institute of Northwestern Washington.

Alcoholics Anonymous World Services. (2001). *Alcoholics Anonymous.* (4th ed.). New York: Author.

Alcoholics Anonymous World Services. (2001). *Alcoholics Anonymous.* (4th ed.). New York: Author.

Alcoholics Anonymous World Services. (2001). *Alcoholics anonymous.* (4th ed.) New York: Author.

Allsop, S., Saunders, B., & Phillips, M. (2000). The process of relapse in severely dependent male problem drinkers. *Addiction, 95*(1), 95–106.

American Psychiatric Association. (2000). *Diagnostic and statistical manual of mental disorders.* (4th ed.—text revision) Washington, D.C.: Author.

American Psychiatric Association. (2000). *Diagnostic and statistical manual of mental disorders.* (4th ed.—text revision) Washington, D.C.: Author.

American Psychiatric Association. (2010). *DSM-5 development.* Retrieved April 8, 2010, from http://www.dsm5.org/ProposedRevisions/Pages/ proposedrevision.aspx?rid=165

American Psychological Association Presidential Task Force on Evidence-Based Practice. (2006). Evidence-based practice in psychology. *American Psychologist, 61,* 271–285.

Angelou, M. (1974). *Gather together in my name.* New York: Random House.

Aubeg, F. R., & Fairbank, J. A. (1992). Behavioral treatment in posttraumatic stress disorder and co-occurring substance abuse. In P. A. Saigh (Ed.), *Posttraumatic stress disorder: A behavioral approach to assessment and treatment* (pp. 111–146). Boston: Allyn & Bacon.

Briere, J., & Scott, C. S. (2006). *Principles of trauma therapy: A guide to symptoms, evaluation, and treatment.* Thousand Oaks, CA: Sage Publications.

Brown, S., & Gilman, S. (2008). *Utilizing an integrated trauma treatment program (ITTP) in the Thurston County Drug Court program: Enhancing outcomes by integrating an evidence-based, phase trauma treatment program for posttraumatic stress disorder, trauma, and substance abuse.* La Mesa, CA: Lifeforce Trauma Solutions.

Burana, L. (2009). *I love a man in uniform: A memoir of love, war, and other battles.* New York: Weinstein Books.

Chilcoat, H. D., & Breslau, N. (1998). Investigations of causal pathways between PTSD and drug use disorders. *Addictive behaviors, 23,* 827–840.

Clancy, S. (2010). The trauma myth. *Psychotherapy networker, 34(2),* 34–39.

Connors, G., & Maisto, S. (2006). Relapse in the addictive behaviors. *Clinical Psychology Review, 26,* 107–108.

Cottler, L. B., Compton, W. M., Mager, D., Spitznagel, E. L., & Janka, A. (1992). Posttraumatic stress disorder among substance users from the general population. *American Journal of Psychiatry, 149,* 664–670.

Courtis, C. A., & Ford, J. D. (2009). *Treating complex traumatic stress disorders: An evidence-based guide.* New York: The Guilford Press.

Curran, L. (2010). *Trauma competency: A clinician's guide.* Eau Claire, WI: PESI.

Dayton, T. (2000). *Trauma and addiction: Ending the cycle of pain through emotional literacy.* Deerfield Beach, FL: Health Communications, Inc.

Delmonico, D., & Griffin, E. (2007). Problematic online sexual behavior. In M. Jarvis, L. Baxter, & J. Tanner (Eds.), *Ruth Fox course for physicians* (pp. 189–221). Miami, FL: The American Society of Addiction Medicine.

Donovan, D. (1996). Assessment issues and domains in the prediction of relapse. *Addiction, 91,* S29–S36.

Duncan, B. L., Miller, S. D., Wampold, B. E., & Hubble, M. A. (Eds.) (2009). *The heart and soul of change: Delivering what works in therapy.* 2nd ed. Washington, DC: American Psychological Association.

El-Sheikh, S., & Bashir, T. (2004). High-risk relapse situations and self-efficacy: Comparison between alcoholics and heroin addicts. *Addictive Behaviors, 29(2004),* 753–758.

Emerson, D., & Hopper, E. (2011). *Overcoming trauma through yoga: Reclaiming your body.* Berkeley, CA: North Atlantic Books.

Erikson, E. H. *Childhood and society.* New York: Norton, 1950.

Erikson, Erik H. *Identity and the life cycle.* New York: International Universities Press, 1959.

Evans, K., & Sullivan, J. M. (1995). *Treating addicted survivors of trauma.* New York: The Guilford Press.

Fletcher, K. E. (1996). Childhood posttraumatic stress disorder. In E. Mash & R. Barkley (Eds.), *Child psychopathology* (pp. 242–276). New York: Guilford Press.

Fosha, D. (2000). *The transforming power of affect: A model for accelerated change.* New York: Basic Books.

Fosha, D., & Slowiaczek, M. I. (1997). Techniques to accelerate dynamic psychotherapy. *American Journal of Psychotherapy, 51*(2), 229–251.

Fullilove, M. T., Fullilove, R. E., Smith, M., Michael, C., Panzer, P. G., & Wallace, R. (1993). Violence, trauma, and post-traumatic stress disorder among women drug users. *Journal of Traumatic Stress, 6,* 533–543.

Golden, K. B., & Bergo, B. G. (Eds.) (2009). *The trauma controversy.* Albany, NY: The State University of New York Press.

Granfield, R. & Cloud, W. (1999). *Coming clean: Overcoming addiction without treatment.* New York: New York University Press.

Grey, E. (2008, September). EMDR theory exists: An explanation of neuro-physiological underpinnings. Workshop presentation at the Annual EMDR International Association Conference, Phoenix, AZ.

Grof, S. (1991). *The holotropic mind: Three levels of consciousness and how they shape our mind.* New York: Harper Collins.

Herman, J. L. (1992). *Trauma and recovery.* New York: Basic Books.

Hernandez, J. T., & DiClemente, R. J. (1992). Emotional and behavioral correlates of sexual abuse among adolescents: Is there a difference according to gender? *Journal of Adolescent Health, 13,* 658–662.

Hien, D., Litt, L. C., Cohen, L. R., Miele, G. M., & Campbell, A. (2009). *Trauma services for women in substance abuse treatment: An integrated approach.* Washington, DC: American Psychological Association Press.

Howell, E. (2008). *The dissociative mind.* New York: Routledge.

Joseph, J., Breslin, C., & Skinner, H. (1999). Critical perspectives on the transtheoretical model and stages of change. In J. A. Tucker, D. M. Donovan, & G. A. Marlatt (Eds.), *Changing addictive behavior* (pp. 160–190). New York: The Guilford Press.

Kabat-Zinn, J. (1994). *Full catastrophe living: Using the wisdom of your body and mind to face stress, pain, and illness.* New York: Dell Publishing.

Keane, T. M., & Wolfe, J. (1990). Comorbidity in post-traumatic stress disorder: An analysis of community and clinical studies. *Journal of Applied Social Psychology, 20,* 1776–1788.

Keller, S. M., Zollner, L. A., & Feeny, N. C. (2010). Understanding factors associated with early therapeutic alliance in PTSD treatment: Adherence, childhood sexual abuse history, and social support. *Journal of Consulting and Clinical Psychology, 78*(6), 974–979.

Kessler, R. C., Sonnega, A., Bromet, E., Hughes, M., & Nelson, C. B. (1995). Posttraumatic stress disorder in the national comorbidity survey. *Archives of General Psychiatry, 52,* 1048–1060.

Kulka, R. A., Schlenger, W. E., Fairbank, J. A., Hough, R. L., Jordan, B. K., & Marmar, C. R. (1990). *Trauma and the Vietnam War generation: Report of findings from the National Vietnam Veterans' Readjustment Study.* New York: Brunner/Mazel.

Levine, P. (1997). *Waking the tiger—Healing trauma.* Berkeley, CA: North Atlantic Books.

Levitin, D. (2006). *This is your brain on music: The science of a human obsession.* New York: Plume/Penguin.

Lisak, D. (1993). Men as victims: Challenge cultural myths. *Journal of Traumatic Stress, 6,* 577–580.

MacLean, P. D. (1990). *The triune brain in evolution: Role in paleocerebral functions.* New York: Plenum Press.

Marich, J. (2009). EMDR in addiction continuing care: Case study of a cross-addicted female's treatment and recovery. *Journal of EMDR Practice and Research, 3*(2), 98–106.

Marich, J. (2010). EMDR in addiction continuing care: A phenomenological study of women in recovery. *Psychology of Addictive Behaviors, 24*(3), 498–507.

Marich, J. (2011). *EMDR made simple: 4 approaches to using EMDR with every client.* Eau Claire, WI: Premier Education & Media.

Maxfield, L. (2007). Current status and future directions for EMDR research. *Journal of EMDR Practice and Research, 1*(1), 6–14.

Miller, D. & Guidry, L. (2001). *Addictions and trauma recovery: Healing the body, mind, and spirit.* New York: W.W. Norton.

Moos, R., & Moos, B. (2006). Rates and predictors of relapse after natural and treated remission from alcohol use disorders. *Addiction, 101,* 212–222.

Mozak, H.M. (2000). Adlerian psychotherapy. In R. J. Corsini & D. Wedding (Eds.), *Current psychotherapies* (pp. 54–98). Belmont, CA: Thomson Wadsworth.

Najavits, L. (2001). *Seeking safety: A treatment manual for PTSD and substance abuse.* New York: The Guilford Press.

Najavits, L. (2006). Present- versus past-focused therapy for post traumatic stress disorder/substance abuse: A study of clinician preferences. *Brief Treatment and Crisis Intervention,* 6:248–254.

Najavits, L. M., Weiss, R. D., & Shaw, S. R. (1997). The link between substance abuse and posttraumatic stress disorder in women: A research review. *American Journal on Addictions, 6,* 273–283.

Norcross, J. (2002). *Psychotherapy relationships that work: Therapist contributions and responsiveness to patients.* New York: Oxford University Press.

Nouwen, H. (2004). *Out of solitude.* (30th anniversary edition). Notre Dame, IN: Ave Maria Press.

Nowinski, J., & Baker, S. (2003). *The twelve-step facilitation handbook.* (2nd ed). Center City, MN: Hazelden.

Ouimette, P., & Brown, P. J. (2002). *Trauma and substance abuse: Causes, consequences, and treatment of comorbid disorders.* Washington, DC: American Psychological Association Press.

Parnell, L. (2007). *A therapist's guide to EMDR: Tools and techniques for successful treatment.* New York: W.W. Norton & Company.

Pearlman, L. A., & Courtois, C. A. (2005). Clinical applications of the attachment framework: Relational treatment of complex trauma. *Journal of Traumatic Stress, 18*(5), 449–459.

Peirce, J.M., Kindbom, K. A., Waesche, M. C., Yuscavage, A. S. E. & Brooner, R. K. (2008). Posttraumatic stress disorder, gender, and problem profiles in substance dependent patients. *Substance Use & Misuse, 43*(5), 596–611.

Perry, B. D., & Szalavitz, M. (2010). *Born for love: Why empathy is essential—and endangered.* New York: Harper.

Prochaska, J., Norcross, J., & DiClemente, C. (1994). *Changing for good: The revolutionary program that explains the six stages of change and teaches you how to free yourself from bad habits.* New York: William Morrow.

Resnick, H. S., Yehuda, R., & Acierno, R. (1997). Acute post-rape cortisol, alcohol abuse, and PTSD symptom profile among rape victims. In R. Yehuda & A. C. McFarlane (Eds.), *Psychobiology of posttraumatic stress disorder* (vol. 821; pp. 433–436). New York: New York Academy of Sciences.

Rothschild, B. (2000). *The body remembers: The psychophysiology of trauma treatment.* New York: W. W. Norton & Company.

Scaer, R. (2005). *The trauma spectrum: Hidden wounds and human resiliency.* New York: W. W. Norton & Company.

Shapiro, F. & Forrest, M. (1997). *EMDR: The breakthrough "eye movement" therapy for overcoming stress, anxiety, and trauma.* New York: Basic Books.

Shapiro, F. & Solomon, R. (2008). EMDR and the adaptive information processing model: Potential mechanisms of change. *Journal of EMDR Practice and Research, 2*(4), 315–325.

Shapiro, F. (2001). *Eye Movement Desensitization and Reprocessing: Basic principles, protocols, and procedures.* (2nd ed.) New York: The Guilford Press.

Solomon, M. F. & Siegel, D. (2003). *Healing trauma: Attachment, mind, body, and brain.* New York: W.W. Norton & Co.

Stewart-Grey, E. (2008). De-stress: A qualitative investigation of EMDR treatment. *ProQuest Dissertations & Theses: Full Text.* (UMI No. 3329984).

Stewart-Grey, E. (2008, September). EMDR theory exists: An explanation of neuro-physiological underpinnings. Workshop presentation at the Annual EMDR International Association Conference, Phoenix, AZ.

Tapert, S., Ozyurt, S., Myers, M., & Brown, S. (2004). Neurocognitive ability in adults coping with alcohol and drug relapse temptations. *The American Journal of Drug and Alcohol Abuse, 30(2),* 445–460.

Terr, L. (1991). Childhood traumas: An outline and overview. *American Journal of Psychiatry, 148,* 10–20.

Turner, S. W., McFarlane, A. C., & van der Kolk, B. A. (1994). The therapeutic environment and new explorations in the treatment of posttraumatic stress disorder. In B. A. van der Kolk, A. C. McFarlane, & L. Weisaeth (Eds.). *Traumatic stress: The effects of overwhelming experience on mind, body, and society.* (pp. 537–558) New York: The Guilford Press.

Ursano, R. J., Fullerton, C. S., Epstein, R. S., Crowley, B., Kao, T-C, Vance, K., Craig, K. J., Dougall, A. L., & Baum, A. S. (1999). Acute and chronic posttraumatic stress disorder in motor vehicle accident victims. *American Journal of Psychiatry, 156,* 589–595.

Van Der Kolk, B. (2003). Post-traumatic stress disorder and the nature of trauma. In M. F. Solomon & D. Siegel (Eds.), *Healing trauma: Attachment, mind, body, and brain* (pp. 168–195). New York: W.W. Norton & Co.

Van Der Kolk, B., McFarlane, A., & Weisaeth, L. (Eds.). (1996). *Traumatic stress: The effects of overwhelming experience on mind, body, and society.* New York: The Guilford Press.

Van Gelder, K. (2010). *The Buddha & the borderline: A memoir.* Oakland, CA: New Harbinger Press.

Walitzer, K., & Dearing, R. (2006). Gender differences in alcohol and substance use relapse. *Clinical Psychology Review, 26,* 128–148.

Walton, M., Blow, F., Bingham, R., & Chermack, S. (2003). Individual and social/environmental predictors of alcohol and drug use 2 years following substance abuse treatment. *Addictive Behaviors, 28,* 627–642.

Weintraub, A. (2004). *Yoga for depression: A compassionate guide to relieve suffering through yoga.* New York: Broadway Books.

Weintraub, A. (2012). *Yoga skills for therapists: Effective practices for mood management.* New York: W.W. Norton & Co.

White, M. (2000). *Narrative means to therapeutic ends: Reflections on narrative practice.* Adelaide, South Australia: Dulwich Center Publications.

White, M. & Epston, D. (1990). *Narrative means to therapeutic ends.* New York: W.W. Norton.

White, W., & Kurtz, E. (2006). *Recovery-Linking addiction treatment & communities of recovery: A primer for addiction counselors and recovery coaches.* Pittsburgh, PA: The Addiction Technology Transfer Center Network.

Yalom, I. (2001). *The gift of therapy: Reflections on being a therapist.* London, England: Piatkus.

Yalom, I., & Elkin, G. (1974). *Each day gets a little closer: A twice-told therapy.* New York: Basic Books.

16413275R00087

Made in the USA
Charleston, SC
19 December 2012